D0262544

Herbert Columbine VC

Herbert Columbine VC

Carole McEntee-Taylor

Pen & Sword
MILITARY

First published in Great Britain in 2013 by
Pen & Sword Military
an imprint of
Pen & Sword Books Ltd
47 Church Street
Barnsley
South Yorkshire
S70 2AS

ISBN: 978-1-78159-309-7

A CIP catalogue record for this book is available from the British Library.

Typeset in 11pt Ehrhardt by
Mac Style, Beverley, E. Yorkshire

Printed and bound in the UK by CPI Group (UK) Ltd, Croydon, CR0 4YY

Pen & Sword Books Ltd incorporates the Imprints of Pen & Sword Aviation,
Pen & Sword Family History, Pen & Sword Maritime, Pen & Sword Military,
Pen & Sword Discovery, Wharncliffe Local History, Wharncliffe True Crime,
Wharncliffe Transport, Pen & Sword Select, Pen & Sword Military Classics,
Leo Cooper, The Praetorian Press, Remember When, Seaforth Publishing
and Frontline Publishing.

For a complete list of Pen & Sword titles please contact
PEN & SWORD BOOKS LIMITED
47 Church Street, Barnsley, South Yorkshire, S70 2AS, England
E-mail: enquiries@pen-and-sword.co.uk
Website: www.pen-and-sword.co.uk

Contents

Herbert George Columbine
No. 50720 Private
9th Squadron Machine Gun Corps
Date of Act of Bravery: 22 March 1918

'For most conspicuous bravery and self-sacrifice displayed, when, owing to casualties, Private Columbine took over command of a gun and kept firing it from 9.00 am till 1.00 pm in an isolated position with no wire in front. During this time, wave after wave of the enemy failed to get up to him. Owing to his being attacked by a low flying aeroplane, the enemy at last gained a strong footing in the trench on either side. The position being untenable, he ordered the two remaining men to get away, and though being bombed from either side, he kept his gun firing and inflicted tremendous losses. He was eventually killed by a bomb which blew up him and his gun. He showed throughout the highest valour, determination and self-sacrifice.'

Acknowledgements

Without the following people it would not have been possible to write the book so I would like to thank them for all their help assistance and encouragement.

First and most importantly, thank you to Michael Turner and the Columbine Statue Fund Committee for giving me the opportunity to write about such a brave man and to Pete Frost for allowing me to use several of his original photos and for also spending ages improving the quality of some of the other photos and images. Pete has a wonderful archive of photos of Walton which you can see at http://www.putmans.co.uk/oldwalton index.htm

I would like to thank Jean Pemberton for the picture of her grandmother Drusilla Dundan, Emma Columbine's sister and the wonderful picture of Emma, and Graham Sacker from the Machine Gun Corp (Old Comrades Association) who has kindly allowed me to reproduce letters and eyewitness accounts of Herbert's heroic last stand.

I would like to thank Keith Langridge for putting me in touch with the South African Military Historical Society SAMHS and to Mrs Joan Marsh, Hon Secretary/Treasurer SAMHS for allowing me to use the images from their website about the battle of Silkaatsnek.

I would also like to thank Keith Packwood for his help in finding me a trench map of Hervilly Woods in WW1.

Last, but definitely not least, I would like to thank Dame Judi Dench for taking the time and trouble to write a Foreword to the book.

Foreword

By Dame Judi Dench

This biography of Herbert (Bertie) Columbine, VC is much more than just the story of his life. After all, he was only twenty-four when he died. This is a veritable history lesson and tells the story of the kind of world into which Herbert Columbine was born, lived and died.

When Bertie's father was born in 1865, it was a very different world to the one in which his son died, but they both gave their lives fighting for their country. How tragic for Bertie's mother to lose both husband and son in such circumstances.

This is a fascinating account of a young man who never knew he was a hero, and the kind of world that made him the man he became. A memorial is long overdue and I hope this account will help achieve that in time to mark the centennial anniversary of the First World War.

Judi Dench

Prologue

Walton-on-the-Naze
March 1918

Afterwards Emma would always wonder why she'd had no premonition of what was to happen. Not that it would have made any difference of course. Bert would have been dead just the same but... Her thoughts tailed off as they always did when she reached the part where Annie, the post woman, had knocked on the door. In glorious ignorance Emma had rubbed her hands quickly dry on her apron and, totally unsuspecting, had gone to answer it.

She'd not even seen Annie walking along the road towards the house because she'd been busy out the back putting the washing through the mangle. She knew Annie quite well. Since the beginning of the war the number of post women had rapidly increased as more and more men were called up to fight and Annie had been delivering her letters for over a year now. It was one of the things she liked about living in the small seaside town. Most people knew each other, by sight, even if not by name. When she knocked on the door, as the postman or woman always did to let you know the post had arrived, they would always exchange pleasantries and Annie would invariably ask how Bert was.

Even when she saw Annie standing there in her uniform, the blue serge coat and waterproof skirt fighting against the wind and the blue straw hat threatening to blow away in the strong gale that was blowing off the sea, she still had no idea. She'd actually smiled at her even as her brain was slowly registering the letter in the brown envelope.

Annie's arm was outstretched, her eyes full of sorrow as she handed it to her, but even then she still had no idea. It was almost as if the world had stopped and even though the sight of the brown envelope with War Office stamped on the front struck terror into any family whose loved ones were serving in the war, it was as if her brain refused to move forward into the present.

As if in a trance she took the letter. She was vaguely aware that Annie was reaching out to her, but she no longer saw her. From being paralyzed her brain had catapulted her abruptly back into the present and she realized that her hands were shaking. She could never remember shutting the door or even walking into the sitting room. But somehow she must have found her way to her chair and sat down. How long she sat there before opening the envelope was another mystery. It seemed like hours but was probably considerably less. Perhaps she had known after all, otherwise why delay so long. It could have said that he was injured and in hospital, but somehow she knew that it didn't. By not opening it she could pretend for a few more precious minutes that everything was the same. That one day the door would open and her beloved Bertie would come home, resplendent in his smart blue uniform, a beaming smile on his face and give her a big hug.

She closed her eyes and tried to picture his face in her mind. For some reason she couldn't. The image of him that had kept her going for so long refused to appear. In its place was darkness, a blank space that was more chilling than any War Office letter could be. Her eyes jerked open in shock and as if in a trance she looked down at the letter which was now resting on her lap. It seemed so innocuous, a small square of brown paper and yet its power to hurt and wound was infinite. She took a deep breath and tried to pull herself together. Fanciful thoughts were not going to help her now. Somehow she had to try and find the strength to open it.

With shaking hands she tore the envelope open and pulled out the contents. At the top was written Army Form B 104-82. The words danced across the page and she had to blink several times before she could focus:

Madam,

It is my painful duty to inform you that a report has been received from the War Office notifying the death of No. 50720 Private Herbert George Columbine of 9 Squadron Machine Gun Corps (Cavalry) at Hervilly Woods on the 22nd March 1918.

The report is to the effect that he was killed in action. By His Majesty's command I am to forward the enclosed message of sympathy from Their Gracious Majesties the King and Queen. I am at the same time to express the regret of the Army Council at the soldier's death in his country's service.

I am to add that any information that may be received as to the soldier's burial will be communicated to you in due course. A separate leaflet dealing with this subject is enclosed.

I am,...

But Emma could no longer read the words which were swimming in front of her. The impersonal form slid gently out of her fingers and floated, unnoticed, to the floor by her feet. She stared sightlessly ahead, no longer seeing the cosy chairs, elegant fireplace and other familiar items that normally gave her so much pleasure. There were no words to describe how she was feeling. No words could possibly describe the pain that was so raw, so unbelievably harsh, that it was in danger of eating away her very soul. It was not enough that the country had taken her husband all those years ago. It had now taken her only son as well.

Oh, she would put on a brave face, the same as she had all those years ago when her Bert had died. But then she'd had young Bertie to keep her going. She'd had to be brave as he'd only been six when his father had been killed in action in the Boer War. With only the two of them she'd had to find a way to get them both through it. That way had been to impress on him what a hero his father had been.

But now there was nothing left, no one to get up for, to work for or to live for. No one to be brave for anymore. She was on her own. Finally the tears began to fall, silently at first and then with considerable force, the sobs wracking her body as she began to rock back and forth, inconsolable in her grief. A grief so terrible that she thought her heart would break.

Chapter 1

1901: My Father, the Hero

Herbert George Columbine, Bert to his friends and Bertie to his mother, stared up at the high ceiling of the tiny bedroom and thought about his father. He was very proud of him for being a hero, honestly he was. But deep down he couldn't help wishing that he hadn't been a hero. Then he would still be here. This thought was always followed by feelings of guilt. He knew his father wouldn't want him to think that. He knew that because his Mum was always telling him how proud he should be of his father who had died bravely for his country. His father, who had been a Private in the 2nd Battalion, The Lincolnshire Regiment and who had been killed in a battle at Zilikaats Nek on 11 July 1900.

He turned over, closed his eyes tight and tried hard to remember what his father looked like. It was such a long time since he'd seen him and although he didn't tell his Mum, he sometimes struggled to remember his face. He could remember little things like how big his father had seemed and how happy they had all been. Then it had all suddenly changed. He could remember his mother shouting at his father one night just before he went away and how sad she had looked the next day. His father had gone away then and it had seemed ages before he came back again although it probably wasn't that long. He had tried to cheer her up, but when he had asked what was wrong, she had just shrugged and said something about his father being stupid and that he was old enough to know better. It was his Grandmother who had told him that his father had gone to be a soldier. For some reason she hadn't seemed very happy either. Bertie couldn't understand it. Everyone at school was really excited about the war and Bertie couldn't wait until he was old enough to go too. But that was women for you.

He did think that his mother would have been pleased to see his father when he had come home to say goodbye. He had looked really smart in his new khaki trousers, tunic, puttees and khaki Wolseley helmet with his Lee-Metford rifle at his side. But she just seemed really sad and he was sure he had heard her crying. Bertie had never seen or heard his mother cry before and he had felt the first stirring of unease. If his mother was crying maybe war wasn't such a good thing after all. The thought had worried him as it was so at odds with everything that he heard at school and in the streets where he played with his friends. Most of the games they played nowadays were war games with the British always beating the wicked Boers of course.

It had worried him so much he had asked his father but he had just laughed and told him that women didn't understand. It was a man's duty to go to war to protect his country and his family. He wouldn't have wanted a coward for a father would he? Bertie had shook his head in horror and thrown his arms round his father's waist, burying his head in the rough serge material of his uniform so he couldn't see that he was near to tears. The thought that he wouldn't see his father for some time had suddenly struck him but he didn't want him to think he was a sissy.

As if sensing his tears his father had then begun to tell him stories about the army, about the exciting places he would see and the adventures he would have. Bert soon forgot his fears. It all sounded really exciting and as he listened he couldn't understand why his Mother had been so annoyed with his father. That night he'd gone to sleep dreaming of the day when he too could join the army, see the world and have lots of adventures just like him. But of course his father had never said anything about people getting killed and not coming home.

The last time he had seen him was early the next morning. His last memory was of his father lifting him high in his arms and swinging him around as he told him not to worry, that he would soon be home again. Bert had looked at his mother's face and then back at his father who had smiled and whispered loudly that he shouldn't worry, she would soon stop being cross with him.

As this thought formed in his mind Bert felt the familiar feel of tears on his cheeks and he quickly turned over, screwed up his eyes and covered them with his hands in a vain attempt to stop them. His father wouldn't want him to cry, he would say he was a sissy, at least that's what his Mother said when he started to cry. She was very brave, she never cried. Even when they had given her the piece of paper saying his father was dead, she hadn't cried. Instead she had hugged him fiercely to her, so tight he had started to struggle. But she had only held him even tighter and eventually he had stopped wriggling and begun to feel frightened. As if realizing this she had loosened her grip and holding him at arm's length she had said firmly, 'You have to be really brave now Bertie. This piece of paper says...' she stopped as she tried to find the words that a six year old would understand. She started again 'It says that your father was a very brave man and...' Again she stopped, unable to say the words that would make it real. 'Your father's not coming back anymore Bertie, he was in a big battle and he was shot by the bad men and...' She still couldn't bring herself to say it.

'Is he dead?' Herbert had asked before she could say anymore.

'Yes, Bertie.' His Mum had pulled him to her again and neither of them had said anything else. Bert had loads of questions but somehow, with a wisdom beyond his years, he knew now was not the time to ask.

The memory of that conversation played over and over in his mind for several weeks afterwards, as did the questions. Who were the bad men? Why had they killed his father? Had anyone punished them? But there never seemed a right time to ask so at night they would go round and round his little mind until eventually he fell into an exhausted sleep.

A few months later when they had talked about the Boer War in a lesson he had asked the teacher to show him the place where his father had died. He had spent quite a long time staring at the place called South Africa on the big wall map that was covered in pink which denoted the extent of the British Empire. To him it seemed as if the British Empire stretched across nearly all the world and he felt very proud to be British. But it didn't make the hurt go away or stop him wishing his father hadn't died.

The 2nd Boer War or South African War had officially started 'at tea time'[1] on the 11 October 1899. The British public assumed it would be a quick victory and be over 'before Christmas' but it proved to be the largest war since the Napoleonic Wars.

Although the politicians were enthusiastic for the war the British army was underfunded, undermanned and hopelessly ill equipped. In those days training was still minimal, three weeks a year was spent on field training and route marches while the rest was spent parading, polishing equipment and pipe laying. Officers were invariably amateurs who had private means and many did not take the profession too seriously. Military intelligence was an even poorer relation and hopelessly underfunded. The Intelligence and Mobilization Division only employed seventeen officers, costing £11,000 while the Transvaal Republic spent ten times this amount.

In the end the war lasted nearly three years, cost £222,000,000 and of the 450,000 troops involved 22,000 died, three quarters of them from disease.

The origins of the war went back to the seventeenth century. The Dutch East India Company (DEIC) had established a small settlement, mainly farmers, (Boers in Dutch) on the Southern Cape of South Africa in 1652. The community had thrived and as they grew they began to demand more independence over making their own laws and deciding to who they should sell their produce. When the DEIC went bust the Dutch government took over control of the Cape until 1795. By then the French had already over run Holland so the Prince of Orange signed it over to Britain rather than have it fall into French hands. The Treaty of Armiens ended the conflict in 1802 and the Cape returned to Dutch control.

But four years later the French were again at war with most of Europe so sixty-three British ships sailed into Simon's Bay and secured the port to ensure the route to India remained open. In 1814 when Napoleon was once again in exile the Prince of Orange demanded the restitution of all the Dutch colonies. But Britain was determined to maintain the routes to the east so refused to hand over the Cape. Eventually, in 1815 under The Act of the Congress in Vienna, Britain paid the Dutch £6,000,000 for the Cape. So after 162 years the Boers had still not gained their independence and they now found themselves under British rule.

As the years went past resentment grew and was fuelled even more by the Emancipation Act in 1834 which deprived them of their black slaves. Eventually they decided enough was enough, and in the two years from 1836–1838 a quarter of the population, over 16,000 Boers, began the long trek north. Some settled between the Orange and Vaal rivers and founded the Orange Free State. Others continued north and then split into two groups. One group went east over the Drakensberg mountains to Natal while the other group went further south eventually settling between the Vaal and Limpopo rivers. Here they founded the Transvaal Republic.

The British annexed Natal in 1843, but in 1852 they recognized the Transvaal Republic through the Sands River Convention. In 1854 they recognized the Orange Free State through the Bloemfontein Convention. For the next twenty years things were reasonably peaceful, but then in 1877 the relationship between the Transvaal and the Zulus began to deteriorate. Fearing a war between them would cause major rebellions elsewhere, particularly in the south, the British annexed the Transvaal Republic. At the time there was virtually no opposition as the Transvaal Republic was more or less bankrupt and in no position to defeat the Zulus on their own.

However, once the Zulus were defeated in 1879, the Boers decided they no longer needed the British and began campaigning once again for their independence. One of these campaigners was Stephanus Johannes Paulus Kruger who would later become President.

Back in Britain in 1880 it was election time and one of the campaign issues of Gladstone's Liberals was the condemnation of what they called 'the insane and immoral policy of annexation'. When Gladstone narrowly defeated Disraeli and won the election the Boers were delighted thinking this would mean they would have their independence at last. But once in power Gladstone reversed the Liberal's policy leaving the Boers feeling they had no choice other than to rebel.

The Transvaal War in 1881 lasted three months and the British were heavily defeated at Bronkhorstspruit, Ingogo River, Laings Nek, and Majuba Hill. At the Treaty of Pretoria in August the British recognized Transvaal Independence other than some rather vague clauses about suzerainty[2] and control of foreign affairs, and everything settled down again. But not for long.

Five years later gold was discovered on Witwatersrand and this bought a massive influx of foreigners into the Transvaal, including many from Britain. By 1890 the 'Uitlanders' began to outnumber the Boers. Determined to prevent the 'Uitlanders' from becoming too strong the Boers kept them under control by taxing them heavily and denying them full citizenship rights. The Uitlanders appealed to Britain for help but were ignored, so they began to consider an armed uprising. Seeing an opportunity to increase British influence in the Transvaal, Cecil Rhodes, Prime Minister of the Cape Colony, was quick to offer his support. He promised to send in a party of mounted police commanded by Dr Leander Starr Jameson, an administrator of the British South Africa Company. However, at the last minute, spies warned Rhodes that the majority of Uitlanders did not actually want an armed revolt. Realizing the cause was lost he pulled out. But Jameson refused to change his plans, convinced that if he crossed the border the revolt would still happen. So, on the 29 December 1895, he and his men crossed into the Transvaal.

The raid was an unmitigated disaster. Once into the Transvaal they headed towards Johannesburg while an advance party was sent to cut the telegraph lines. But in their haste they overlooked a branch line. This meant Kruger knew exactly where they were and was able to mobilize local commandos to set up an ambush.[3] On 1 January 1896 Piet Cronje set up an ambush at Krugersdorp in which Jameson lost thirty men, either killed or wounded. The remainder surrendered after a disastrous attempt to outflank the Boers and ended up in Pretoria jail.

Three years later the Uitlanders again appealed to Britain for help, this time sending a petition to Parliament stating their grievances. The British Commissioner Sir Alfred Milner met President Kruger to discuss the problems, but the meeting was a failure and the situation rapidly deteriorated.

With the backing of President Steyn of the Orange Free State, Kruger issued an ultimatum to Britain demanding several things: that Britain give up suzerainty, withdraw troops from the Transvaal border, remove all reinforcements from South Africa within a reasonable time, set up an arbitration committee to settle their differences and give assurances that the troops en route to the Cape would not be landed. These conditions were to be complied with by 5pm on the 11 October 1899.

Their demands were rejected and on the 12 October the Boers attacked Cape Colony and Natal. The main Transvaal force under Commandant-General Joubert crossed at Laing's Nek. They then split into two wings, one to the east and the other to the west and entered Natal at Botha's Pass and Wool's Drift. Further east Commandant Lukas Meyer crossed the Buffalo River at De Jager's Drift while the Orange Free Staters crossed the Drakensburg Mountains through Van Reenan's Pass and Tintwa Pass to the West and approached Ladysmith. Heavily defeated at Talana Hill and Elandslaagte the British army of 13,000 men were forced to retreat back to Ladysmith, Kimberley and Mafeking where they were then besieged.

On 14 October General Sir Redvers Buller, who was Commandant in Chief of South African Forces, sailed from Southampton to join the 47,000 men of the South Africa Field Force who were advancing on Cape Town. On arrival he divided his forces in three and while the left flank advanced on Kimberley, the centre flank headed towards Stormberg. Those on the right flank established a camp at Frere, twenty-five miles from Ladysmith where they prepared to relieve the town. The three British offensives that followed at Stormberg, Magersfontein and Colenso between the 10 and 17 December in 1899 were such a disaster that it became known as 'Black Week'. The news was received back home with horror and disbelief and Britain went into shock.

Chapter 2

Changing Times

Herbert Edward Columbine, Bertie's father, was born in October 1865 in Islington, the son of Mark Columbine and Sarah Clarke. At the time of his birth his father was a tailor in Islington.

Emma Royal, Bertie's mother was born in Brandon in Suffolk in about 1856 to Robert and Harriet Royal. Robert was a maltster[1] and the family moved around through Suffolk, Norfolk and Cambridgeshire. In 1861 the family were living at 31 Church Walk in Brandon, Suffolk. At that time Emma had an older brother Henry who was fourteen, three older sisters, Harriet Ruth and Anna Maria who were both twelve and Charlotte Elizabeth who was seven. Emma was six and she also had a younger brother, Robert, who was three and a baby sister, Drusilla, who was two months old. Emma went into service and at the age of sixteen the 1871 census finds her living at 116 Brandon Road in Lowestoft as a servant to Mary Plumb and her nephew Edward G C Snare.

In January 1872, a Robert Royal, with the same date of birth as Emma's father, was tried at Ipswich and found guilty of a 'felony as a receiver' and given two years hard labour. In July 1872 Robert Royal died in the Ipswich district.

The 1881 census finds Emma living in 10 Redcliffe Street, St Mary's in London as a servant to John and Elizabeth Shallis. In the same year her mother Harriet is listed as a lodger at 66 Yeomans Row in Kensington and her profession is listed as needlewoman.

From this it would seem that there had been considerable changes to the Royal family's life. But it was not just the Royals who were facing change. There had also been massive changes in the country during the nineteenth

This is the census document showing where Emma Royal, Herbert's mother, lived as a child, with her parents and siblings.

century. The world into which Emma and Herbert Edward had been born was noticeably different to the world in which their son Herbert George would be born, towards the end of the century.

At the beginning of the century most people lived in the country and worked in farming. By the end of the century the majority of the population lived in towns and cities and worked in some kind of manufacturing. The population of Britain had grown from nine million in 1801 to forty-one million by 1901 despite over fifteen million people emigrating between 1814 and 1914. By 1881 the population of London alone was 3.3 million. Whilst the people were still trying to adjust to these massive social and economic changes, their lives were also affected by external factors such as the Long Depression.

The period known as the Long Depression was a worldwide depression that began in 1873 and lasted to almost the end of the century. Its effects were worse in Europe and the USA but although it was a period of low growth and general deflation it was later considered to be not as bad as that of the Great Depression of the 1930s. However Britain was considered to have been hardest hit as it began to lose its lead over the industrial

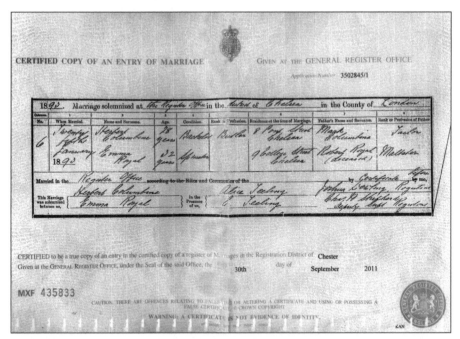

A copy of the marriage certificate of Emma Royal and Herbert Columbine (snr).

economies of Europe. This created difficult social conditions and massive social and political changes.

Early nineteenth century families had eaten a diet based predominately on bread, butter, potatoes and bacon. But as railways and steamships began importing more food from abroad diets improved considerably. Being able to import cheap grain from North America reduced the price of bread and the invention of refrigeration meant cheap meat from Argentina and Australia became available.

However, the importation of cheap grain and meat had an adverse effect on the farming community. Falling food prices created rural unemployment and encouraged workers to move to the overcrowded towns and cities in their thousands. Their arrival eroded employment, wages and working conditions of those already there.

Conditions in towns and cities were very unsanitary with unpaved streets and uncollected rubbish which was allowed to accumulate until it rotted. It was then used as fertilizer. Only the rich had flushing toilets in the early nineteenth century while the poor used cesspits, which were not emptied very often. Alternatively they shared toilets with other families leading to long queues. These unsanitary conditions led to outbreaks of cholera in 1831–32 and again in 1848–49. In 1886 over 17,000 people died of a cholera outbreak, 6,000 in London alone. In 1872 the Public Health Act was set up to appoint medical health officers and sanitary authorities and by the late nineteenth century most towns had dug sewers and there were piped water supplies leading to much healthier conditions. As the century progressed more people had flushing toilets.

But poverty was rife and was believed to be the fault of those suffering it. If you had no income you were sent to the workhouse where families were separated and conditions were as unpleasant as possible to dissuade people from asking for state help. However, as the century progressed, attitudes had slowly begun to change.

In 1878 William Booth formed the Salvation Army and in the 1890s teachers began providing free breakfasts of bread, jam and cocoa to children who were malnourished. In the same year boot funds were started to provide shoes and boots to children who previously had been barefoot. The legal age of consent remained at twelve years old up until 1875 when it was finally raised to thirteen. But as many children had no idea how old they were it was easy for them or others to lie about their age.

Housing began to improve over the century as regulations were brought in to control how close dwellings could be built to each other and to govern the size of rooms and windows. However, by the end of the nineteenth century, overcrowding was still common with far too many families still living in one room in old houses which were divided into separate dwellings. Landlords did little in the way of repairs and upkeep and holes in broken windows were often stuffed with paper or rags. Homelessness had risen dramatically by the end of the century and hundreds of people were sleeping rough in the Royal Parks and Trafalgar Square. In 1885 the Royal Commission on the Housing of the Working Classes made public the poor housing conditions in London although little was done to address the problems.

The winter of 1885/1886 was the worst in living memory with snow falling continuously from October to May. This added to the economic problems. Even in London people didn't escape as a foot of snow fell on the capital in just seven hours in January 1886.

A copy of the London schools admission register showing Herbert age six registered for Woodland Road School.

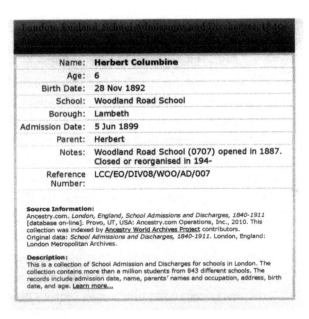

London, England, School Admissions and Discharges, 1840-

Name:	**Herbert Columbine**
Age:	6
Birth Date:	28 Nov 1892
School:	Woodland Road School
Borough:	Lambeth
Admission Date:	5 Jun 1899
Parent:	Herbert
Notes:	Woodland Road School (0707) opened in 1887. Closed or reorganised in 194-
Reference Number:	LCC/EO/DIV08/WOO/AD/007

Source Information:
Ancestry.com. *London, England, School Admissions and Discharges, 1840-1911* [database on-line]. Provo, UT, USA: Ancestry.com Operations, Inc., 2010. This collection was indexed by Ancestry World Archives Project contributors. Original data: *School Admissions and Discharges, 1840-1911*. London, England: London Metropolitan Archives.

Description:
This is a collection of School Admission and Discharges for schools in London. The collection contains more than a million students from 843 different schools. The records include admission date, name, parents' names and occupation, address, birth date, and age. Learn more...

As unemployment rose so did fears about the radicalization of the working classes. About eighty per cent of the population during the nineteenth century was considered to be working class. Only those who could afford at least one servant were judged to be rich enough to describe themselves as middle class.

In 1886 riots and strikes became more common leading to the Black Monday riots in London. The 13 November 1887 became known as Bloody Sunday as 2,000 police and 400 troops were deployed in Trafalgar Square to prevent demonstrations against various issues getting out of hand. Although marched into position the Infantry did not open fire nor did the Cavalry draw their swords. But in the ensuing clashes with the police many were injured, including women and children and there were three fatalities.

Strikes continued over the next two years with the Bryant and May match girls strike of 1888. This was followed by the dock strike of 1889, but the attention of most people in the capital was now concentrated on the Whitechapel murders which had begun in August 1888. In January 1890 a global flu pandemic hit London causing many deaths and a certain amount of panic. But Emma's fortunes appear to have changed as from being a lowly servant in 1881 the 1891 census finds her living at 44 Everest Street in

Chelsea with her mother and sister Charlotte. The census further states they had a furniture business.

For some working people things had begun to improve and by the late 1880s some lived in houses that had two rooms downstairs and two or even three upstairs. For skilled workers conditions were even better. They often had houses with flushing toilets and a scullery with a copper container for washing clothes. Water and soap powder was added to the copper and the clothes were turned with a wooden tool called a dolly or pushed up and down with a metal plunger which had holes in it. Wet clothes were then wrung through a mangle to dry them. By the end of the century many working class homes had become much more family orientated. With more family-centred homes came a need for possessions with which to fill them, including furniture. It was this that may have enabled Harriet, Emma and Charlotte to set up a furniture business.

At the beginning of the nineteenth century most families had cooked over an open fire but in 1820 iron cookers called ranges were introduced. By the mid-nineteenth century most families were cooking on ranges and towards the end of the century many had boilers behind their coal fires which enabled them to heat their water.

Carpet sweepers were invented in 1876 and by this time most people had gas lights even if it was just downstairs. Upstairs would often still be lit by oil lamps. By the 1880s gas fires had become more common and by the 1890s gas cookers became much more affordable. Although electric light was gradually introduced[2] to light streets it was expensive and took a long time to replace gas lighting in homes. The first electric street lights appeared in London in 1878.

Bathrooms were only for the rich in the early nineteenth century, but by the 1870s and 1880s the middle class began having bathrooms built, their water heated by gas. Working people had tin baths and washed in front of the kitchen range, something that would continue for some time.

There was also a much greater selection of food available by the latter part of the century. Margarine was invented in the 1870s and tinned food became more widely available in the 1880s. Consumption of sugar also increased and several new biscuits were invented: the Garibaldi in 1861, cream crackers in 1885 and digestives in 1892. Peanut brittle was invented in 1890 followed by liquorice allsorts in 1899. Although chocolate had always been a popular drink the first chocolate bar was not actually invented until 1847. Milk chocolate was invented even later in 1875.

It had also been much later in the century that there had been any discernable difference to womens' lives. At the beginning of the century, as soon as they were old enough, they had either worked on farms or as servants. The majority of servants were women as their wages were cheaper than those of men. Later in the century work on the farms and being 'in service' was exchanged for work in factories.

Even when they married and had children women's lives were often not any easier. Contraception was unheard of and many women spent year after year giving birth. Infant mortality was high, as was death from childbirth. As many as half of brides were pregnant at their weddings and many people could not afford to get married at all so just lived together.

In 1869 John Stuart Mill had published a book demanding equal rights for women called *The Subjection of Women*. At the time women were very much an underclass as far as the law was concerned. In 1870 the Married Woman's Property Act allowed women to keep £200 of their earnings, inherit personal effects and small amounts of money but anything else, regardless of whether they owned it before or after marriage, belonged to her husband. It was not until 1884 that a further Married Women's Property Act made her a person in her own right, rather than a chattel of her husband. This was followed in 1886 by The Guardianship of Infants Act which allowed women to become sole guardians of their children if their husbands died.

Divorce had finally been made legal in 1857 but it was very rare in the nineteenth century and those who did divorce were considered to be outcasts. It was also very one sided. Men could divorce women on grounds of adultery, but women could not divorce men on the same grounds unless they could also prove cruelty, incest, desertion or some other cause.

Attitudes to womens' education did change very slowly though and from 1865 women were allowed to become doctors. In 1884 Oxford University finally allowed women to attend lectures and take exams, but they were not allowed to be awarded degrees until 1920.

Women did not have the national vote, although women ratepayers were allowed to vote in local elections after 1869. New Zealand became the first country to allow women to vote in national elections and that was in 1893.

Women did not normally go out to work unless they were single or widowed however, evidence from family budgets, seems to suggest that women were employed in higher numbers in the 1850s, 60s and 70s that at any time up to the 1950s.

Being 'in service' was a major employer of women. Other common trades were in confectionery, brewing, cleaning and retail. Women were also seamstresses or worked in laundries. But the invention of the telephone (1876) and typewriter (1874) increased the number of work opportunities for women, even though the wages of those who worked outside the home were a third, and sometimes less, of that earned by men.

Once married, women were expected to stay at home and have children. This left many with no option but to take in washing or sewing, or go out cleaning and cooking to supplement their husband's often meagre income. Some resorted to prostitution as the only means of ensuring the children were fed.

There was little real demand for education before 1870 and it is unclear whether either Emma or Herbert would have been taught to read as children. The higher classes were reluctant to educate the poor through fear of revolution and the poor needed the income their children earned so were reluctant to send them to school. In the early and mid part of the century the church began to provide some education and after 1870 those areas which did not have church schools were provided with non denominational state schools. If parents couldn't afford to pay school fees the state would pay for a limited time. But the 1870 Act did not make education for children compulsory.

The factory system had long since replaced people working in their own homes, but conditions were dreadful, until a succession of acts was passed to govern how women and children should work. In 1833 the law ruled that children aged nine to thirteen must not work longer than a twelve-hour day or forty-eight-hour week and those from thirteen to eighteen should not work more than sixty-nine hours a week. Night work was banned for those under eighteen and children aged nine to thirteen were given two hours of education every day. In 1842 the law was extended to ensure that those under ten and all women should no longer work underground and this was followed in 1844 by a ban on all children under eight from working. By 1847 The Factory Act was changed to ensure that women and children could no longer work more than ten hours a day in the textile factories. This was extended to all factories that employed more than fifty people in manufacturing in 1867. In 1875 the practice of sending boys up chimneys to clean them was finally outlawed.

It was the 1876 Royal Commission on the Factory Acts which recommended education for children should be made compulsory to prevent child labour. But it wasn't until 1880 that another Education Act made attendance at school compulsory for those between the ages of five and ten. This did not do much to enforce attendance as by the early 1890s about eighty-two per cent of children were still failing to attend. It wasn't until 1891 that fees were abolished.

When Herbert married Emma Royal in 1893 he was working as a butler at 8 Pond Street in Chelsea and Emma was living at 9 College Street, also in Chelsea. On the wedding certificate she is listed as 'spinster'. This may be because women's occupations were not always listed or because she was not working at that time. Their witnesses were an Alice and C. Teeling. The wedding took place in January 1893 in Islington and Herbert George was born the following November. The family continued to live in London and work in the furniture trade, presumably the business that Emma was already working in with her sister and mother.

In 1893, the year Bertie was born, compulsory attendance at school was extended to the age of eleven and six years later it was extended to the age of twelve. Despite this the Columbines appear to have moved around while Bertie was young and he appears to have changed schools three times. He first appears on the admission register of St Andrew's Roman Catholic School Polworth Road, Lambeth with an admission date of 20 April 1896, aged three. The family were then living at 60 Colmer Road. Although the family moved to 1 Colmer Road Bertie remained at the same school until the 24 February 1897 when the family left the neighbourhood to move to Streatham. Here Bertie attended St Leonards School until the 2 November 1898 when he was again removed. By the 5 June 1899 the family were living at 44 Anersly Road and Bertie began attending the Woodland Road School in Lambeth.

With the increase in literacy reading had become very popular in the nineteenth century. The first detective story, *The Murders in the Rue Morgue*, was published by Edgar Allen Poe, and *A Study in Scarlet*, the first Sherlock Holmes story, was published by Arthur Conan Doyle in 1887. Musical evenings were popular with middle class families who would spend many evenings gathered round a piano and singing. Even more popular were the Music Halls with their variety of performers which really came into their own towards the end of the nineteenth century. Newspapers also became widely available as the century progressed, thanks to the invention of the steam driven press in 1814 and the abolition of stamp duty in 1855 which made them cheaper. This bought the news to people who previously would have had little access to country or world affairs.

Although only about eight per cent of the adult male population who were old enough for military service were involved in the Boer War, the rest of the nation soon became caught up in 'Khaki fever'. The main reason behind this was that this was the first war in which pictures could be seen.

Henry Fox Taylor had taken the first photograph in 1835 and the first cheap camera had been invented in 1888 by George Eastman. The cartridge film from the Pocket and Bullet Kodaks of 1896, and the cheaper Brownie, which became available from 1900, made the war accessible to people in a way in which it had never been before. The strong South African sunlight made the quality of the pictures extremely good and this also brought the war into people's lives in a way that had never been previously possible. Added to the still pictures were those of the bioscope which showed moving pictures to the audiences in the music halls. W K-L Dickson, a naturalized American, was the leader of a band of professional photographers whose pictures were shown to audiences the length and breadth of the country. This brought the war right into their lives and although some of the photos were staged, and others were obviously artificial, it still made the war real to millions of people who otherwise would have been almost unaware of it.

In addition to pictures and film there were also lots of stories and poems in circulation. These were often written by soldiers on active duty. But for the first time it was not just the words of educated officers. Soldiers of all ranks were writing letters, poems and stories about their experiences, because by then most soldiers were literate. Arthur Conan Doyle, who was extremely popular by then, even wrote a history of the war while it was still going on.

The invention of the telegraph in 1837 meant that news reached Britain almost immediately. The newspapers carried their own stories about the war, many including letters from the soldiers on the front line. This would be the last war in which letters from war zones were uncensored.

On 16 December 1899 a call for British volunteers was published in the papers. Many of the volunteers came from the upper working class and lower middle classes. Most were tradesmen, clerks and shop workers who had received basic elementary education and left school at around twelve years of age. Against this background of nationalistic fervour and shock at the defeats that were so unexpected, many men left their professions, their wives and their children and rushed to join the army. One such man was Herbert Edward Columbine, Bert's father.

As the war news continued to deteriorate Kipling's *Absent Minded Beggar* began to be recited every night by Mrs Beerbohm Tree in the music halls. Music was added by Arthur Sullivan and over a quarter of a million pounds was raised for soldiers' families. Another music hall favourite was Will Dalton and F J Willard's *A Hot Time in Transvaal Tonight*. When the troops left their towns and villages to go to war thousands lined the streets to cheer them off. It was estimated that half a million people cheered off the troops from Southampton, while vast crowds lined the streets when the City Imperial Volunteers set off.

As war fever continued and Emma tried to pick up the pieces of her life, alone and with a growing son to feed, Herbert Edward Columbine happily completed his training and prepared to leave for South Africa. He and the rest of the 2nd Battalion (10th Foot) the Lincolnshire Regiment sailed on the *Goorkha* on the 4 January 1900 and arrived in Cape Town on 27 January 1900. The Lincolnshire volunteers were to follow, leaving Southampton on the *Guelph* on the 17 February. It would take until June for them to catch up to their parent unit.

Chapter 3

Silkaatsnek

W hile Herbert prepared to leave England and Emma and Bertie continued without him, events in South Africa had moved on. General Sir Redvers Buller had compounded his previous errors by sending a message to General Sir George White in Ladysmith telling him to fire off all his ammunition and surrender. This was the final straw for the politicians and in London the decision was made to remove him. On 10 November his replacement, Field Marshal Lord Roberts, arrived in Capetown. He was accompanied by his Chief of Staff, Lord Kitchener of Khartoum. Meanwhile the 5th Division, commanded by General Sir Charles Warren, had also arrived in South Africa. This increased Buller's strength to over 30,000 men. Without a firm strategy in mind he made the decision to hand over the operation to relieve Ladysmith to Warren. Warren advanced on the southern hills overlooking Tugela, but despite several attempts was unable to take Tabanyama Hill which overlooked the road to Ladysmith. With Buller's reluctant approval, he then decided to attack Spion Kop, a disastrous decision that left 1,200 of his men wounded, killed and captured while the Boer casualties numbered only around 300.

On arrival in South Africa Roberts and Kitchener had immediately set about removing the dependence on the railways by organizing mule wagons. Although this may have been a good long term strategy, in the short term it caused some severe supply problems with men on the front line running out of even the most basic items, including boots, medical supplies and fresh water. The situation was made worse when Christiaan de Wet captured 200 unprotected supply wagons at Waterfal Drift on the Riet River on the 15 February.

Fortunately Major General John French had retained his own transport and he made a dash for Kimberley, successfully relieving the town on the 15 February. The Boer Commander, General Piet Cronje retreated along the railway line to join de Wet where his force was engaged by Kitchener. The Battle of Paardeberg was inconclusive and very costly, leading to the loss of most of the British cavalry.

Meanwhile the substantial mounted force Roberts had put together arrived and by mid February he had outflanked Kimberley. A demoralized General Piet Cronje and 4,000 men finally surrendered on 27 February. The following day the Boers withdrew from Ladysmith and were attacked by the South Africa Field Forces at Poplar Grove on the 7 March. Despite the decisive defeat of the Boer forces President Kruger and his commandos were allowed to escape. The advance continued and when Bloemfontein in the Orange Free State fell with suprising ease by the 13 March it encouraged Roberts into thinking that Boer resistance was over. On 17 May the siege of Mafeking was finally relieved after 217 days and on the 5 June 1900 Roberts entered Pretoria. Still believing the Boers were a spent force Roberts offered an amnesty for everyone except the leaders if they would lay down their arms. For the soldiers it really seemed like the war was over and they would soon be home.

The Battle of Diamond Hill, ten miles east of Pretoria which took place on the 10 and 11 June, was the final straw for the Boers. After their defeat they disappeared into the wilderness north of the Magaliesberg. Believing the war was more or less over the Western Transvaal burghers surrendered Rustenburg to Lt Col R S S Baden-Powell and then retreated to the area around Bronkhorstspruit-Balmoral.

Once Pretoria had fallen on the 5 June the British commanded most of the strategic points, but their communication and supply lines stretched back hundreds of miles through the inhospitable country of the Western Transvaal. For the troops the conditions were extremely difficult to fight in. The ground was hard and full of stones making digging in difficult. Sources of water were few and far between while viscous barbed bushes scratched their limbs and tore at their clothes, leaving their uniforms in tatters. There were numerous steep hills that were difficult to take and even harder to defend and by now the British troops were severely depleted and thinly spread. In addition they had to struggle with equipment, baggage, cavalry, artillery and various other support services.

In contrast the Boer fighters were extremely tough horsemen and marksmen who knew the territory and were used to the conditions. They were also highly mobile and needed little in the way of support. They could not defeat the British by frontal assaults or by set piece battles, instead their strength lay in other directions. Before long they realized that their knowledge of the local terrain made guerrilla warfare the perfect option.

On the 11 July the Boers attacked in four places, all of them successful. One of these was at a place called Silkaatsnek (also known as Zilkaatsnek or Nidal's Nek) and one of the first casualties was Herbert Edward Columbine.

Silkaatsnek was a U-shaped gap in the Magaliesberg range, a single mountain range which formed a natural barrier that extended a little way north of Pretoria and a further 100 miles (160km) to the west. Because of the sheer cliff face on the southern side there were only certain places that wheeled traffic could get over it, the seven or so passes or Neks which would become of great tactical importance in the campaign of the Western Transvaal. One of these was Silkaatsnek, seventeen miles west of Pretoria.

The Magaliesberg was about 1,300 feet (396m) above the plain whilst Silkaatsnek was only 350 feet (107m) high. The Nek itself was divided in two by a kopje, an elongated rocky outcrop. The road the vehicles used to travel over the Nek ran alongside the western side of the outcrop. Once at the summit of the slope the road passed through a twenty-five yard cutting in the Nek alongside the kopje which itself overlooked the pass by about seventy-five feet. The mountains on either side were even higher and overlooked the pass. On the eastern side they rose steeply, but the rise was more graduated on the western side. Here there was a deep gully on the northern slope which almost separated it from the main range.

The northern face offered several places to climb as long as the troops avoided the gullies and ravines caused by centuries of erosion. But there was a sheer cliff on the southern face which could only be climbed in very few places on foot and even fewer places on horseback. Whereas the northern side was covered in thick bush the south was more sparsely covered except at the cliff base. Here, along the side of the stream in the Silkaatsnek, the bush was again much thicker and the ground covered with a broad sweep of Mimosa trees. The nearest crossing point to the Nek was at Leopard's Kloof, about a mile to the east, and there were concerns that this might allow the Boers to outflank their positions in Silkaatsnek. They were right to be concerned.

General De la Rey now commanded the northern sector of the Boer Forces including the Western Transvaalers. Having realized that their only hope of success was to change tactics and resort to guerrilla warfare he took 200 of his men and went back to Bronkhorstspruit-Balmoral to reorganize and reinforce the Western Transvaalers. Whilst travelling north of Silkaatsnek on his way back to Rustenburg he was informed by his scouts that the Nek was only lightly held and that the commanding shoulders, the high ground, had been ignored. Seizing the opportunity to show what could be done De la Rey decided to attack.

There were 1,500 men and two batteries at Silkaatsnek and Commando Nek under the command of Baden-Powell. The 2nd Dragoons, Royal Scots Greys, commanded by Lt Col the Hon W P Alexander Bart were under instructions to relieve the Neks which Baden-Powell had stressed should be held at all costs. They were located at a cavalry outpost called Derdepoort on the railway line some four miles north of Wonderboom Fort.

Meanwhile, on the evening of the 6 July, Baden-Powell had been ordered west to support Major Hanbury-Tracy's Rustenburg garrison against 400 Boers who were threatening to overrun it. In turn the Royal Scots Greys were due to be relieved by the 7th Dragoon Guards on the 7 July. However, there was a mistake in the orders. The words '3.5m south of Waterval' had been omitted and the Dragoon Guards did not arrive at Derdepoort until noon. This delayed the departure of the Royal Scots Greys.

After leaving one section of the second gun with the Guards, 'O' Battery, Royal Horse Artillery, commanded by Major Sir J H Jervis-White, Bart, the Royal Scots Greys and 50 Australian Horse decided to save time by taking the direct road to Rustenburg. This traversed the exposed northern side of the Magaliesberg. The dust thrown up by their movements could be seen for miles and high on the top of the Magaliesberg the Boers watched silently as the troops headed towards the Neks. But they did not have time to gather sufficient numbers to mount an attack, so for the moment they just watched and waited.

The Scots Greys had already crossed this territory once after the Battle of Kalkheuwel Pass on their way to Pretoria on the 5 June. On the way through they had left 'A' Squadron to occupy Silkaatsnek. The Royal Horse Artillery (RHA) had followed a day later. But although they all found themselves retracing their earlier steps it was now a month later and very dark by the time they reached Silkaatsnek. 'C' Squadron, which consisted of Major H J Scobell, Capt C J Maxwell, Lt T Conolly and eighty men and two guns of 2nd Section 'O' Battery under Lt W P L Davis, were sent to hold the Nek while the main party continued for another three and a half miles over Silkaatsnek to Crocodile River. By the time they arrived it was freezing cold, their transport had not turned up and the only shelter they could find was a deserted shop.

On the following morning, the 8 July, 'B' Squadron Scots Greys and the Maxim machine gun crossed the bridge over Crocodile River and after two miles reached Commando Nek. Meanwhile Headquarters, 'A' Section of the Greys, the 50 Australian Horse and 3rd Section RHA moved two miles in the opposite direction to Rietfontein. Baden-Powell's fortified communications post at Rietfontein was near the western end of a long series of low hills and covered the river (two miles away) and the passes of Commando Nek (just under five and a half miles away) and Silkaatsnek (just over three miles away). It was in permanent heliographic and telegraphic communication with Pretoria.

Herbert Edward Columbine and the 10th Foot The Lincolnshire Regiment under Col H R Roberts left Pretoria on Tuesday 10 July. Their orders were to relieve the cavalry who were needed to help clear the Boers from south and west of the Magaliesberg. They too knew the area as on the 15 June they had marched the exact same road, rested at Rietfontein and continued the long ten mile trek to Commando Nek arriving on the 17 June. They had left 'C' Company there while the Battalion had gone on to Pretoria. Here it had remained since the 20 June.

Continuous fighting, numerous casualties, lack of replacements and equipment had taken their toll on the Lincolnshire Regiment and at least five Companies were under strength. It was a seventeen mile march back to Silkaatsnek from Pretoria and they reached the foot of the Nek late in the afternoon on the 10 July. The rear guard, 'G' Company, together with 'D' and 'F' Companies and their Maxim machine gun, who were to go on to Commando Nek arrived at 16:30. This was about half an hour before sunset. Too tired to go any further, they pulled up half a mile to the rear and bivouacked next to the road, ready to continue their march the next day. Because it was nearly dark there was very little time to reconnoitre the area properly.

Col Roberts was carrying orders from Pretoria instructing Col Alexander at Rietfontien to take three squadrons westward to join Col H L Smith-Dorrien. He travelled first to Rietfontien to hand over these orders before heading back to Silkaatsnek. This meant he was the last to arrive, by which time it was completely dark.

When he had first occupied the Nek, Major Scobell had divided his Squadron in two. Fifty-five of his seventy-five available men were deployed about a third of the way up either side of the shoulders of the Nek, with the two guns placed in the gap east of the kopje. To protect the guns sangars[1] were built and wire entanglements were placed in front of them. However their field of fire was severely restricted as the bush in front of them had only been partially cleared to a distance of 200 yards. Major Scobell (Scots Greys) had not appreciated being left at the Nek as he considered it would be a difficult position to hold and that the guns would probably be more hindrance than help. He had also warned Col Alexander in Pretoria by heliograph of a possible attack by De la Rey and upwards of 1,600 Boers. But nobody at Rietfontein believed that the Boers would attack 'C' Squadron, even when his warning was endorsed by Col Roberts who had also sent a message to Pretoria requesting reinforcements, when he took over from Major Scobell.

As they were leaving the next morning Col Roberts withdrew the Scots Greys south of the kopje where they spent the night sleeping in columns, their rifles by their sides. They had left their horses in the bush at the bottom of the Nek.

After dark at 1830hrs 'G' Company, which consisted of thirty men under Captain Edwards, and half of 'A' Company set up sentry posts for the night. Some were placed facing north on the road towards Rustenburg while eighteen men and a Colour Sergeant were placed on the right of the northern entrance to the Nek. Concerned about a possible flank attack by way of a mountain footpath the rest of 'A' Company under Capt J J Howley were sent to the right to cover the rear. 'B' Company under Lt G F Prichard remained with the Scots Greys in reserve in the centre. Probably because there was a deep rocky gully to the north-west of their positions they mistakenly assumed it was impassable. Thus the western side was not occupied at all.

The night was dark and bitterly cold with temperatures dropping to near zero, although it may have felt slightly less cold because of the dry air and lack of wind. This was in total contrast to the hot dry heat of the day in which the sun had shone down forcefully raising temperatures to above 20 degrees C. Because there was little wind the dust and smoke from bush fires had considerably impaired visibility, especially through the day. But that night the full moon was shining brightly lighting up the area quite well.

Despite this, during the hours of darkness, 200 Boers managed to creep into position after climbing up the mountain over night. By dawn they were positioned on both shoulders, their orders to wait for the guns to fire twenty shots before attacking. Commanders De Beer and Visser were in charge of those on the east, while Commanders Coetree, Kirtsen and Boshoff waited with their men on the west.

But things did not entirely go to plan. Accounts as to the exact time vary but it would seem that at dawn or first light firing could be heard from the Lincolnshire sentry posts on the right. There had been no bombardment; it appeared the sentry post had been surprised. After a few brief moments of intense fighting they were surrounded and forced to surrender. They had lost four men. Several more moments elapsed before the Boers on the east began firing, but when they did their guns could be clearly heard at Rietfontein.

As with most accounts of battle detail varies but what was clear was that all hell broke loose as the sentry post on the right fell back to the centre while the rear guard came forward to support the guns. At first the bullets flew harmlessly overhead as the Scots Greys climbed the eastern end of the kopje and began firing on the Boers advancing from the right. Seeing the Boers working their way across the front to the left twenty men and one officer were then ordered to reinforce the left flank.

The men with ammunition wagons and artillery horses on the right were not so lucky. They had much further to go to find shelter from the bullets and after covering only about thirty yards the Boers had found the range, killing and wounding at least seven men and most of the horses and mules.

There was not enough time to use the machine guns as the increasing rifle fire meant the machine gunners had to keep their heads below the level of the sangar. This made it impossible to service the guns. Although they did manage to fire shrapnel and all eight rounds of their case at the advancing Boers they were unable to get sufficient elevation to counter the fire from the Boers, who now held the eastern heights thus dominating the gun sangars.

Things moved so quickly that they were unaware that the Boers were already on top of the western buttress which overlooked the kopje. Needing to occupy the western buttress to be able to fire on the eastern side Lt Pritchard and 'B' Company found themselves in a fierce fire fight as they sought to take the high ground. The British force on the kopje now found themselves caught in murderous crossfire between the Boers on the south-west and those occupying the north-east. Because the north-east was well wooded it provided ample cover for the Boers to creep up on the defenders.

Gradually they advanced forward attacking not only the centre but also on the right of the left sentry post.

Fire was now coming from all around them and the British were forced to retreat, taking cover where they could find it in the bush that bordered the road and stream. In their haste to reach cover 'A', 'B' and 'G' Companies left the heliograph in the camp and despite several attempts to reach it were not able to do so until just before sunset. This meant they were not able to send for the reserves from Rietfontein and Commando Nek.

No communication with the Nek also meant there was no forward observation post and no way to correctly gauge the strength of numbers against them. The fighting continued unabated and then the Boers bought up a Vickers-Maxim, two field guns and two one-pounder Maxim Nordenfeldts (pom-poms) and began attacking the kopje. At the same time the fire from both the east and western buttress increased as the Boers steadily advanced from all sides.

Col Roberts did manage to get a message through to Colonel Alexander asking for artillery support. But after several hours Alexander withdrew his guns concerned about shelling his own men and also worried the guns would fall into the hands of the Boers. The besieged men fought on. They were desperately short of ammunition and water but were told reinforcements were on their way. However, these reinforcements from Pretoria who had been expected at 1500hrs, failed to arrive. They had not set out until 1400hrs and although they included 450 mounted infantry, 500 infantry and four guns they were still six miles from the Nek at 1600hrs. At 2000hrs they met up with Alexander's men coming back the other way and then the entire force returned to Pretoria.

For the abandoned men there were few options left. It was a bright moonlit night making it virtually impossible to escape unseen. They had also taken considerable casualties. Eventually they had no option but to surrender.

The Boers considered their casualties to be substantial with eleven dead including De la Rey's nephew, eight wounded, two seriously. The Imperial forces lost twenty-two killed, with a further four Lincolnshire's dying later from their wounds. The Lincolnshire dead were buried at the foot of the Nek the following day. (Their remains were later re-interred at Rietfontein in 1972.) The figures for those wounded vary, but was believed to be around fifty-one with approximately 158 being taken prisoner.

But for Bert the figures meant very little other than the fact that one of the dead was his father.

Chapter 4

'God Save the King'

Thanks to the telegraph news reached home very quickly and by 17 July 1900 it was obvious that Britain had suffered another massive defeat in South Africa. At first the news meant nothing to Emma. Although she'd received quite a few letters from Herbert telling her all about South Africa and the fighting, she had no real idea of where he was.

The first letter had arrived not long after he had left and had been written whilst on board the ship. It had begun with a description of them all singing songs on board the ship as it had sailed out of Southampton and how they had finished with a rousing rendition of 'God Save the Queen'. The picture he'd painted had bought tears to her eyes as she visualized all the men watching their homes and families fade into the distance as the ship sailed away. The next few days had been spent trying to get through the Bay of Biscay. Caught up in a massive storm the winds had blown to gale force, the rain had pummelled the decks and the ship had pitched and rolled leaving most of the men with seasickness and unable to get out of their hammocks. Lucky enough not to be stricken by seasickness Herbert had spent some time on deck watching the sailors as they fought to control the massive ship against the even more immense forces of nature. Once out of the Bay it appeared things had improved considerably and he had gone on to describe their day with so much detail that she almost felt as if she were there.

The day began at 6am as they were woken and, as there were so many of them, was swiftly followed by the struggle to find space to wash. With the ship rolling as it rode the large waves of the open ocean they would then try and shave, an activity that left many covered in bits of cotton wool and plaster. As she read this, Emma found herself smiling. Trying to imagine

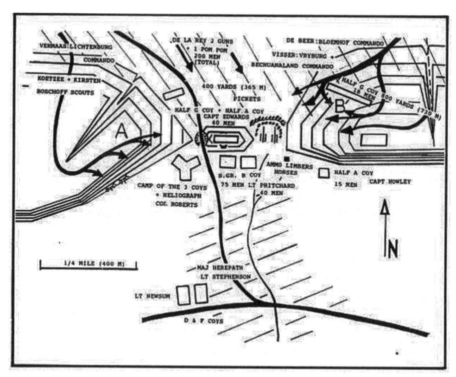

A map showing the positions of both Boers and British soldiers on the night of July 10th to sunrise on July 11th.

them stumbling around whilst doing their best not to cut themselves was quite funny especially as Herbert was very particular about his shave. Selling furniture meant his appearance was very important so he always took considerable care to present a smart clean scrubbed face to the world. He would have hated to be covered in bits of cotton wool.

Breakfast was at 8am and was haddock or herrings and beef steak, bread and butter and coffee. Parade followed at 10am and here they were divided into different watches while others were sent to clean mess rooms, tidy hammocks and generally clean up. Below decks there were twelve to a table and their hammocks were strung out over the top of their own table at night. Dinner was served at noon and was either soup, pork and currant roll or roast or boiled beef, mutton or pork with potatoes. This was followed by a good selection of puddings. Tea was normally served at 5.30pm and was either bread, butter and jam or marmalade, smoked haddock and kippers, or cold meat and tea.

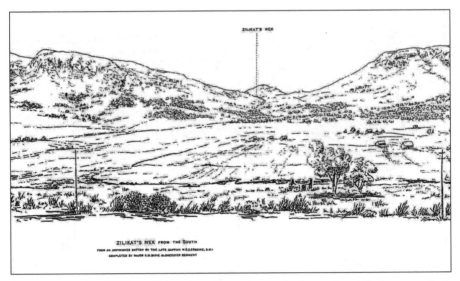

This is a sketch of Zilikats Nek as seen from the south. It was here Herbert snr died.

It seemed they could also buy provisions on board and he had delighted in telling her the special prices they were charged. Lemonade and soda was only 3d a bottle as was cheese and biscuits. Beer was 6d a small bottle and they were allowed one each a day. At night they would sit writing letters, the better educated helping those who might be struggling. There was always a good sing-song to finish the day and then the men would climb into their hammocks to sleep.

The next letter was of a similar vein as it described their excitement at anchoring off Tenerife in the Canary Islands. Although they weren't allowed ashore they were able to buy fruit from the natives who came out to the ship in small boats, as well as tobacco and cigarettes. They had regular sports on board and Herbert boasted of having a very good tan. He also thought he was putting on weight thanks to all the good food he was eating.

As she read his second letter Emma began to feel decidedly cross. Herbert was obviously having a wonderful time while she worked twice as hard to keep their business going and to keep the roof over their head. Yes she would get some of his wages, but that was not really adequate compensation for having to do all the work and having all the responsibility for their son. Much as she loved Bertie a part of her envied Herbert his ability to just change his life on a whim. Having decided to join the army he had not given a thought to the effect it would have on their lives. She sighed heavily and, putting the letter back in the envelope, she placed it in the drawer with the first one. She would answer it later when she was feeling less angry. At least he had given her an address now.

As the months went on he continued to write, but the tone of the later letters was nothing like as jovial as the first ones in which he had struggled to contain his excitement at being on his way to a strange country. They were now punctuated with news about friends who had been wounded or who had died. Many of the longest paragraphs were about trains full of wounded heading back to Cape Town to go home and other trains full of prisoners, unkempt and uncared for.

No longer were they eating like kings as their food was now just bully beef and biscuits and buying extra supplies was expensive. Rations were often just a pound of meat, a loaf and some coffee each day. If they were lucky they had jam twice a week, but their soup often had ants in and there was no butter only dry bread and coffee. As she read this Emma began to feel guilty about having begrudged him the good food he had eaten on the ship.

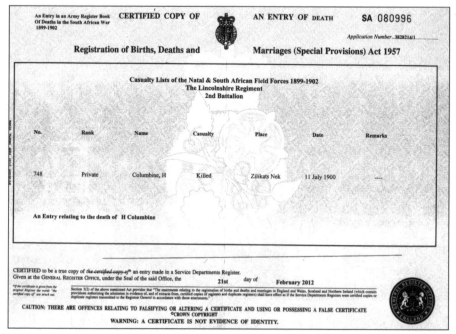

A copy of Herbert snr's death certificate.

Picture of the Boer War Memorial in Lincolnshire Cathedral showing Herbert snr – 2nd column 6th from bottom.

A closer view of Herbert's name on the memorial.

He went on to describe the stifling heat that greeted them every day, the exhausting seventeen mile marches across barren scrub or mealie fields with waist-high grass. He talked about the endless prairies, the thick bush and steep hills they had to climb with enormous packs and sweat pouring down their faces. He described the hot choking dust storms as they foundered across sand and the rushes of icy hail that assaulted them as they reached the summits of hills. The days were stiflingly hot and the nights freezing cold. Equipment shortages were chronic, damaged uniforms were not replaced so they scavenged where they could. Boots wore through and because there were no replacements men had to remain behind whilst the rest went into battle.

The Elgin Commission set up after the war, which reported in the summer of 1903, stated that the war had been a catalogue of errors. When the war first started there had been no maps of the ground over which they would fight. Some of the rifles were wrongly sighted and there was not enough ammunition. While the War Office had plenty of red, white and blue uniforms that were useless in the Veldt, it did not have enough khaki. The Remounts Division was understaffed and under-resourced, as was the Railway Transport Division whose role it was to transport the men and equipment across thousands of miles. When the war started it only had one officer, one batman, one horse and a groom. The Royal Medical Corps collapsed under the strain and intelligence work at all levels was totally inadequate, as was all staff work. The Elgin Report placed the blame squarely on the shoulders of politicians who had either not wanted war at all or had not envisaged a prolonged conflict. It also criticized their policy of prioritizing the Navy at the expense of the army.

But this was all in the future and no help to Herbert and rest of the troops who just wanted to survive long enough to go home. His letters now began to make repeated references to the stifling airless heat and how their water was severely rationed. Looking out at the cold wet streets of London in the early spring of 1900 Emma found it hard to imagine such heat. But the pictures she had seen in the Music Hall bore out his letters and she would often find herself scouring the moving pictures and those in the papers looking for some sign of him.

Although he had still tried to sound reasonably upbeat, despite the continuing shortages of everything, including ammunition and medical supplies, she could tell that he'd had enough. It was no longer the

The 1901 census showing Emma as an employer and her son Herbert.

adventure he had thought it would be and he was longing for the war to be over so he could come home. Emma sighed as she finished reading his latest letter. He really didn't sound very happy at all. She folded it carefully before putting it back in the envelope and then opened the drawer to add it to the others. As she closed the drawer she suddenly had a strange premonition that this would be the last time she ever heard from him. Dismissing it as the foolish fancy of a weak woman she shook herself and went downstairs to make tea. It wouldn't do to let Bertie know she was worried, so she put on a brave face and banished her fearful thoughts to the back of her mind.

Bertie would rush home from school every day to see if there was a letter from his father and when he did get one he was the envy of his friends as he showed off the exotic stamps. Unlike her letters, his were all about the exciting things his father had seen like flying fish, dolphins, porpoises and even an albatross. The later ones described mountains alive with monkeys, vast open spaces and strange natives who wore few clothes. Bertie soaked up the information like a sponge and would rush into school the next day to share it with his friends. He was beside himself with excitement to think his

1901 England Census	
Name:	**Herbert Columbine**
Age:	8
Estimated Birth Year:	abt 1893
Relation:	Son
Mother's name:	Emma Columbine
Gender:	Male
Where born:	Chelsea, London, England
Civil parish:	Penge
Ecclesiastical parish:	St Paul
Town:	Penge
County/Island:	Surrey
Country:	England
Street Address:	
Occupation:	
Condition as to marriage:	
Education:	
Employment status:	
Registration district:	Croydon
Sub-registration district:	Croydon
ED, institution, or vessel:	95
Neighbors:	
Household schedule number:	28
Piece:	650
Folio:	71
Page Number:	4

Household Members	Name	Age
	Emma Columbine	39
	Herbert Columbine	8

The 1901 census showing Herbert as a child.

father had seen all those things and he couldn't wait for his turn to travel the seas and have lots of adventures.

Despite her determination to put aside her worries Emma was unable to shake the impending sense that something was wrong. But not wanting Bertie to see her concern she tried to keep her feelings to herself. Then, as the next couple of weeks passed and the news from South Africa improved she allowed herself the luxury of relaxing. It seemed as if the war might be coming to an end and she began to believe that her premonition that she would never see him again really had been nothing more than a foolish fancy.

Even when the letters stopped abruptly she didn't worry. News of the sinking of *The Mexican* meant some of the mail from South Africa had probably gone down with the ship. So when she heard of the latest disaster to befall the Imperial Army she had no idea that it would have any effect on her. It was only when she saw the headlines proclaiming 'Disaster to the 2nd

The 1901 census showing Emma.

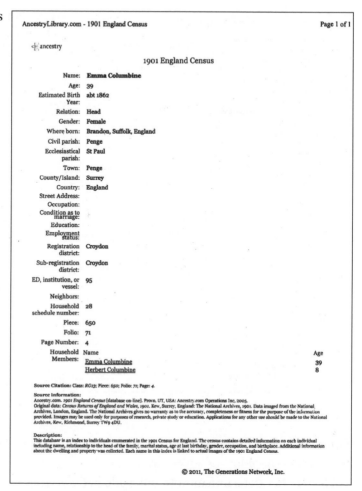

Lincolns' that her heart began to beat faster and she rushed to buy the paper, hoping casualty lists were printed in it. At least that way she could satisfy herself he was not among them. But there were no casualty lists yet just a brief resume of the battle and the number of those killed, wounded or captured.

News informing relatives of individual casualties took considerably longer than it did for news to reach the newspapers. Once casualties were confirmed the War Office would write to those affected giving them the dreaded news. However this could be weeks after the event and so it was likely that Emma would not have heard anything definite until the autumn.

The commercial directory for Beckenham showing Emma as a wardrobe dealer 1902,

PREFACE.

——

The present is the eighteenth annual issue of the
BECKENHAM DIRECTORY.

Every effort has been made to bring it up-to-date.
It is the pleasing duty of the Publisher to acknowledge
his indebtedness to the many residents who have assisted,
by correction and suggestion, to complete the Work, and
he assures his correspondents that communications of a
similar nature will be always welcomed.

January, 1902.

COMMERCIAL DIRECTORY.   195

Chalk, C., baker and confectioner, Elmers End road
Chalk, V. B., fishmonger, poulterer, etc., 12 and 63, High street
Chalk, Vernon B., butcher, Bromley road, and 61, High street
Cherritt, F. P., coffee and dining rooms, 13, Trinity road
Chitty, E. J., dressmaker, 100, Bromley road
Church, Elkana, undertaker, 72, Bromley road
Churcher, E. W., bootmaker, 106, High street
Clamp, F. A., fly proprietor, High street
Clarke, G. W., cycle engineer, 34a, High street
Clarke, Henry, coffee tavern, 55, Parish lane
Claxton, Miss, dressmaker, 5, Manor road
Codlin, F., " George Inn," High street
Cole, J. S., family draper and milliner, 7, High street
Collins, A. E., gilder and picture frame maker, 4, High street
Columbine Mrs., wardrobe dealer, 35, Marlowe road
Coombe, Mrs., stationer, 73, Parish lane
Cooper, F., household stores, 16, Trinity road
Cooper, S. T., watchmaker and jeweller, 5, Pelham road

But by the time she received the official notice she already knew. Herbert had been a surprisingly good correspondent and had written nearly every week. Although she could explain away the lack of letters as being because they were on a ship that had sunk, it would not explain why she had heard nothing for weeks, nothing in fact since the battle in which the 2nd Battalion had suffered so many casualties back in July.

Emma had continued working after Herbert had gone to war. Hard as it was at least she could enjoy the opportunity to remain in one place for longer than a few months. Since marrying Herbert she seemed to have spent her life moving from one part of London to another and she worried

THE

BECKENHAM
DIRECTORY
FOR
1903.

NINETEENTH YEAR OF ISSUE.

COMPRISING

THE WHOLE OF THE DISTRICT

UNDER THE JURISDICTION OF THE

BECKENHAM URBAN DISTRICT COUNCIL

AND

WEST WICKHAM.

With Map, Price Eighteenpence.

Subscribers, One Shilling.

CONTENTS:

BECKENHAM :

PRINTED AND PUBLISHED BY T. W. THORNTON,

AT HIS PRINTING AND BOOKBINDING WORKS,

42 & 44 HIGH STREET.

Entered at Stationers' Hall.

COMMERCIAL DIRECTORY.   189

Caston, P. and E , ladies' outfitters, 15, Albemarle road
Cator Estate Offices, (T. H. Burroughes), 24, Southend road
Caudwell Bros., " Kent House Tavern," Kent House road
Caudwell, A. F., " Park Tavern," Trinity road
Challis, T., Kent House nursery, Beckenham road
Chalk, C., baker and confectioner, 40, High street, and Elmers End road
Chalk, V. B., fishmonger, poulterer, etc., 12 and 63, High street
Chalk, Vernon B., butcher, Bromley road, and 61, High street
Cherritt, F. P., coffee and dining rooms, 13, Trinity road
Chitty, E. J., dressmaker, 100, Bromley road
Church, Elkana, undertaker, 72, Bromley road
Churcher, E. W., bootmaker, 106, High street
Clamp, F. A., fly proprietor, High street
Clarke, G. W., cycle engineer, 34a, High street
Clarke, Henry, coffee tavern, 55, Parish lane
Claxton, Miss, dressmaker, 5, Manor road
Codlin, F., " George Inn," High street
Cole, J. S., family draper and milliner, 7, High street
Coles, T. F., " Railway Hotel," High street
Collins, A. E., gilder and picture frame maker, 4, High street
Columbine, Mrs., wardrobe dealer, 35, Marlowe road
Connelly, H., fishmonger and poulterer, 7, Albemarle road
Coombe, Mrs., stationer, 73, Parish lane
Cooper, F., household stores, 16, Trinity road
Cooper, S. T., watchmaker and jeweller, 5, Pelham road
Cooper, W., watchmaker, 60, Bromley road
Copeland and Son, builders, 9, Bromley road, and New Beckenham
Copper, E., " Jolly Woodman," 9, Chancery lane
Cornwall, E. H., coal merchant, Penge station
Coronation Coffee Tavern Company, Ltd., 71, Beckenham road
Coward, J., bootmaker, 1, Brook place
Cox, Mrs. F., toy dealer, 98, High street
Cox, T., builder, 98, High street
Crawley, Thomas, and Son, bootmakers, 5, Parish lane
Croucher, William, greengrocer, 49, Croydon road
Crown Wine and Spirit Company, 100, Bromley road
Crease, J., fruiterer and greengrocer 43, High street
Cupit and Co., W. W., Oakhill fish stores, 84, Bromley road
Curtis, Cornelius, upholsterer and cabinet maker, High street
Curzon, F. C., confectioner and tobacconist, Elmers End road

The Beckenham directory for 1903.

about the effect it was having on Bertie's schooling. Now on her own Bertie was able to stay at the same school and they had begun to live a more settled life.

They had been living at 44 Anersley Road for over two years now, the longest they had been anywhere since she had married. But Herbert's death meant a large drop in her income and she began to worry about whether she could afford to stay where they were. The last thing she needed now was to have to move and even worse for Bertie to have to move schools again. She had heard that if her husband died his belongings would be sold and she would receive any money from this sale, but that was it. There was no pension or any other money for the dependants of service men killed in action. In 1881 the War Office had turned down proposals to give war pensions to widows and dependants, although they had agreed to give them one year's pay. That was why they had been collecting money for them in the music halls. They could also apply to the Royal Victoria Patriotic Fund. She had heard of other wives and children ending up in the workhouse after

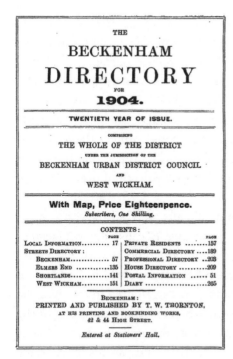

The directory for 1904.

their husbands were killed or having to hastily remarry but she had no intention of having that happen to her. She had her business and Bertie was getting older. Soon he would be able to leave school and start working and things would become easier.

But first she had to find out what had happened to his father and then she had the unenviable task of telling Bertie that his father was probably dead. However, as yet she had no proof, so she would wait for official notification before saying anything.

Although Queen Victoria had sent a telegram to Lord Roberts on the 17 July stating: *'Anxious to hear about the wounded in the most regrettable affair at Nitral's Nek'* signed VRI, the public for the most part had lost interest in the war thinking it to be virtually over. Buller returned to England at the beginning of October closely followed by Roberts. The war limped on for another eighteen months as the Boers changed their tactics from futile frontal assaults to the more successful guerrilla warfare.

To try and limit the range and effectiveness of the Boer commando attacks Lord Kitchener, who was the new Commander in Chief in South Africa, began intensifying the scorched earth policy started by Roberts. This meant burning farms and destroying crops to deny the commandos vital supplies and civilian support. The British then built forty-six camps in which they concentrated the destitute men, women and children made homeless by these policies and in which they could protect the more co-operative Boers. But because of the lack of adequate preparation they soon became insanitary and full of disease and led to the death of over 20,000 of the 117,000 detainees.

On the 22 January 1901 Queen Victoria died after sixty-three years on the throne and the nation was plunged into mourning. Because she was Head of the Army she had left instructions for a military funeral with her coffin drawn by eight horses on a gun carriage. The coffin arrived in London on the 2 February from the Isle of Wight and crowds gathered to watch as the coffin decorated with the Imperial Crown, orb, sceptre and the collar of the Order of the Garter was carried by gun carriage through the streets. It was followed by King Edward VII, Kaiser Wilhelm II, and various other heads of state.

Emma and Bertie stood in the cold February air watching with the rest of London as the coffin went slowly past. For the young Bertie the pomp and ceremony was something he would never forget and the sight of the soldiers in their splendid uniforms lining the streets only fuelled his desire to join the army when he was older. As Emma watched she had no idea how she felt. The sight of so many soldiers was a painful reminder of what she had lost, but she was also drawn into the emotion of the moment, making her alternatively sad yet proud to be British.

At the age of fifty-nine Edward VII had now succeeded to the throne. Queen Victoria had never allowed him to become involved in foreign policy so he relished the opportunities now open to him and threw himself into his role with great enthusiasm.

Back in South Africa in early 1901 Kitchener had introduced the block-house system in which the country was divided into sections with long barbed wire barriers commanded at intervals by command posts or blockhouses from which patrols maintained the security of the wire fences. But despite having established some 8,000 blockhouses extending over 3,700 miles by the end of the war they were only moderately successful.

By the end of 1900 there had been 11,797 casualties in the Boer War leaving 2,359 widows with little money and having to rely on charity. This finally led to the introduction of state pensions in April 1901 for widows and orphans of ordinary soldiers who had been killed on active service. But there were strict conditions and qualifying criteria. The widows and dependants of black soldiers did not qualify, although they could receive discretionary payments. The soldier had to be killed through active service and if the widow remarried or committed 'misconduct' (e.g. having liaisons with other men) she would lose the pension. For Emma the pension was a lifeline and for the first time in ages she was able to stop worrying about money.[1]

She and Bertie had continued to live at 44 Anersley Road since Herbert's death. On the 1901 census Emma is listed as an employer so she seems to have been quite successful at earning a living. Bertie, now eight, was still at the same school and looking forward to the time he could leave. Public interest in the war had waned considerably but Bertie still thought about his father and couldn't wait until he was old enough to join the army himself. Even at his young age he could see that this might not be something his mother would like so he kept it to himself; his big secret.

In South Africa the war carried on despite a proclamation by Kitchener in August 1901 demanding the unconditional surrender of all Boers still under arms. The proclamation was largely ignored leaving a frustrated Kitchener stuck in South Africa instead of being free to take up his post as Commander in Chief in India.

In September 1901 there was a smallpox outbreak in London and the death toll in London by January 1902 had risen to 2,273. This was part of a wider pan-European outbreak that had begun in 1901. There was no vaccination yet for smallpox and Emma found herself watching Bertie like a hawk for any symptoms of the disease. To her relief the number of fresh cases began to drop and as the spring wore on the threat passed. It was to be the last smallpox epidemic in London.

Sporadic fighting continued until early 1902 and then, on the 7 March, 1,300 men under the command of Lord Methuen were attacked by De la Rey at Tweebosch. It was the worst British defeat in the latter stages of the war and left 200 dead with over 600 wounded. Once again the war was back in the headlines reviving sad memories for Emma and strengthening Bertie's resolve to join up and avenge his father.

But it seemed that both sides had now had enough and on the 10 April Schalk Burger, acting President of the Transvaal, and Marcus Steyn, President of The Orange Free State met with Botha, de Wet and De la Rey and agreed to enter peace negotiations with Kitchener. On the 28 May the Boers met to consider the final draft of the peace treaty. After agreeing to lay down their arms and acknowledge Edward VII as their lawful sovereign the treaty promised an amnesty for all except those guilty of war crimes and restoration of all property to prisoners of war who took an oath of loyalty to the King. It further promised equality of the Dutch language in schools and in the law courts, £3 million to help restore and restock the farms that had been destroyed, a promise that no war tax would be levied and transition to self government as soon as circumstances permitted. The Boers were divided over whether to accept the treaty, but it was passed by a huge majority and at 10.30pm on the 31 May 1902 the Treaty of Vereeniging was signed in the dining room of Kitchener's Headquarters. The Boer War was finally over.

Back in England Beatrix Potter published *Peter Rabbit* and Rudyard Kipling's *Just So* stories were published. But of more interest to Bertie was the excitement surrounding the coronation.

In August London was again regaled in pomp and ceremony as Edward VII finally enjoyed his coronation. It had been delayed from July because of the King's appendicitis. Once again Emma and Bertie joined the crowds lining the route in London cheering on their monarch. This time Emma no longer thought about Herbert with the same sadness as before. Business was going well and the extra money from Herbert's pension was helping to make their lives more comfortable. Bertie watched the ceremony with a certain amount of envy. He couldn't wait to be old enough to join up and after seeing the splendid uniforms of the cavalry, their horses freshly groomed and marching in time to the music, Bertie knew exactly which regiment he wanted to join. He didn't want to be infantry like his father and have to walk everywhere. It would be much better to join the cavalry and travel in style.

Emma and Bertie had now moved to 35 Marlowe Road in Lambeth. Here they remained for the next three years with Emma's business as a wardrobe dealer[2] listed in the Beckenham Directories for 1902, 1903 and 1904.

In 1905 Bertie was twelve years old and was now officially old enough to leave school. Emma decided to move. She was fifty and no longer wanted to be working all the time. If she found somewhere cheaper to live the proceeds from the business and Herbert's pension would be more than enough for her to live on. Bertie was now old enough to get a job too so with his wages she could begin to take it easy. With good memories of happy holidays spent at the seaside as a young girl it was perhaps not surprising that once Bertie left school Emma decided to move to Walton-on-the-Naze.

Chapter 5

Walton le Soken

Walton-on-the-Naze, which used to be known as Walton le Soken[1], can trace its history back to before the Middle Ages, but like many coastal towns on the east coast it had fought a continual battle against tidal erosion. The town that existed originally is now situated in the North Sea and its medieval church finally disappeared into the sea in the late eighteenth, early nineteenth century. Historically it was largely a farming community, but there does seem to have been some connection with the sea as in 1342 Walton supplied a ship for Edward III's expedition to Brittany and in 1572 Thomas Colshill, a surveyor of Customs in London, noted that Walton had one ship in the 'under 20 tons' category.

Another rival to agriculture was the manufacture of copperas or green vitriol. Copperas was used for sheep dipping in the thirteenth century and in the eighteenth century for dyeing and tanning and the manufacture of ink. The copperas stones were washed out of the cliffs by the waves and gathered by women and children and taken to copperas houses for manufacture. In 1629 there were two copperas houses in Walton. As the wool and tanning industries in East Anglia declined so did the copperas industry, although some was still sent to Ipswich to be used in the manufacture of sulphuric acid.

Its role as a seaside place seems to have first taken off in the early nineteenth century when in 1815 John Aldridge began advertising the Bath House Hotel followed by his bathing machines. Its population in 1821 was just 293. Brighton had opened its pleasure pier, the first to be built, in 1823 and soon other resorts began to follow suit. In 1829 the first guide to Walton was published and The Hotel opened with its twenty-four sitting rooms and bedrooms, coffee lounge and ballroom. By 1831 the population had grown to 469 after a small pier was built in front of The Hotel in 1830. It was initially built as a landing stage for the steam ships from Ipswich and London but unfortunately it was too short at only 150 feet. It was in the 1830s that the Summer Regatta started which attracted lots of visitors to take part in the rowing and sailing races and other events. Others came just to watch.

In 1840 another guide was published called *An Historical and Geographical Description of the Favourite Watering Hole of Walton-on-the-Naze*. It mentioned the Summer Regatta and the band which was located opposite The Hotel and by 1841 the population had grown still more and had reached 721. In 1848 the pier was lengthened to 330 feet but was still too short for the steam ships.

In 1855 Peter Bruff[2] arrived in the town and began developing the town. In 1859 he built Marine Terrace and South Crescent. He improved the water supply by sinking an artesian well and built a gas works which introduced a gas supply to the town. In 1862 he opened the Clifton Baths which was also known as the Clifton Music Hall which had a 350-seat theatre, reading room, billiard room and indoor baths. He then began building a new pier to rival the old one. Although it had only reached 600 feet by 1880 the old pier had been destroyed by a fierce storm in 1881 so the steam ships had no option but to use his pier. In 1864 he started bringing the railway to Walton, something that was finally achieved on 17 May 1867.

The Bank Holiday Act in 1871 now ensured workers had some paid holidays each year and by the 1870s some workers began to also have a weeks' paid annual holiday and Saturday afternoons off. Thus it was in the 1890s that the weekend was born. Workers had already had Sundays off since the beginning of the century, but the half day on Saturday was now extended to most workers in the 1890s. However, there were still those who had no holidays other than bank holidays. Holidays to the seaside grew in popularity for those who could afford it and Walton became even more popular.

Peter Bruff sold his remaining interests in the town in 1897 to the Walton-on-the-Naze Hotel and Pier Company. This soon went bust and was taken over by the Coast Development Company. It improved the pier by lengthening it to 2,610 feet and making it accessible for steamers. It also built a 750-seat pavilion for shows and concerts. It included rooms for refreshments, the headquarters of Walton swimming club, a shooting saloon and an electric railway which ran the length of the pier.

Other attractions began to grow up around it, and together with sailing and the pleasure boats providing tours round the pier, Walton became a flourishing seaside resort. By the time Emma and Bertie moved to Walton the population was over 2,000.

Their home, 33 South Crescent Cottages, was set back behind the main parade and only a few minute's walk from the sea and about the same from the pier. Bertie was fascinated by the electric train that ran the length of the pier and loved nothing better than watching the passengers alight from the paddle steamer, the *Walton Belle*, as it tied up at the end of the pier. The other activity that attracted lots of interest was watching the men from the life boat as they came in from rescuing those who had got into difficulty.

To Emma's delight the High Street was also thriving with a steam laundry and a variety of shops including bakers, butchers, drapers, fishmongers, a post office and a branch of Barclays Bank located downstairs in the Town Hall which had been built in 1900.

Living was much cheaper in Walton and the pace of life much slower. After the frantic pace of life in London Emma immediately felt at ease, and although it meant leaving his friends Bertie soon settled in. He explored the beach and surrounding areas, made new friends and went for rides on the horse and cart belonging to John William Hipkin, a cartage agent for the Great Eastern Railway.

Bertie also loved watching the antics of the baker's horse as it raced full tilt back from the Naze, the young baker's boy frantically trying to hold him back while the cart veered dangerously from side to side. Bertie had heard that the horse used to be a race horse and didn't take too kindly to being put 'in the traces' hence his unpredictable behaviour. But worse was to come. Arriving back in the town one day, the horse, who was very highly strung and easily startled, suddenly reared up on his hind legs crashing the cart through a glass and china shop window.

Bertie was now old enough to work and it is believed he either found employment on the electric train on the pier or with the Great Eastern Railway. Walton was expanding every year and in the years before the Great War had become very popular with the rich and famous and many of the guests included royalty.

In April 1908 the Territorial Army was formed and once again Bertie felt his familiar longing to join the army, but he still wasn't old enough and in any case nothing but the regular army would really satisfy him. It was also the year the government introduced the Old Age Pension Act. This was 5s a week to single people over seventy whose annual income was under £21 per year. Married couples received 7s and 6d a week.

In 1909 the Liberal Government tried to introduce the so-called 'People's Budget', but it was voted down by the Conservative majority in the Lords. This led to the first reform of the power of the House of Lords in 1911.

By 1911 Emma was living at 33 South Crescent Cottages in Walton le Soken, as it was still known. The winter had arrived late that year bringing

FRINTON AND WALTON DIRECTORY.	
25, Mr. Newby	11, H. J. Halse
RIGHT SIDE.	12, H. Chamberlain
2, R. A. Broad	13, H. J. Wright
4, G. Farrow	14, C. H. Horbuin
6, Mrs. Fairbrother	15, S. J. Canham
8, W. Porter	16, A. J. Meakins
10, E. Mann	
12, H. Candler	First Avenue.
	LEFT SIDE.
Agar Road.	20, W. Garney
Off Church Road.	22, G. Moss
1, Mrs. Bartlett	24, J. Moss
2, P. Oxley	19, Mrs. Stuart
3, B. Osborne	21, A. M. Upson
4, H. Fairbrother	23, H. Kerridge
	25, A. Newstead
Crescent Road.	27, F. Spencer
At Rear of Round Garden.	29, A. Keeble
21, Mrs. Lambert	31, G. T. Paxton
23, A. Gray	33, Mrs. Prime
25, S. Dawson	35, Mrs. Beasley
27, W. James	RIGHT SIDE.
29, J. Hobbs	Homecroft—C. H. Vince
31, H. Britton	1, W. J. Finch
33, Mrs. Columbine	2, G. Chapman
	3, W. C. Minks
East Terrace.	4, D. Ablitt
East Cliff Private Hotel—	5, G. F. Betts
L. Sichel	6, F. Sayers
3 & 3a, Esplanade Hotel—	7, G. Baker
Mrs. A. Sichel	8, R. Herbert
4, F. Bacon	9, J. Keeble
5, R. M. Alexander	10, A. L. Byas
6, A. J. Miles	11, M. Drable
7, E. Johnson	12, J. Kingsley
Douro—H. W. Flateau	13, F. H. Couchman
Helsam—Miss Cross	14, L. Langham
Mount Ephram—S. A. Taylor	15, F. L. Philpott
Bethany—C. Taylor	16, H. Mallott
The Nest—R. F. Garnham	17, W. L. Fowler
	18, J. Mayes
Eagle Avenue.	
1, W. C. Albany	Green Lane.
2, A. D. Gray	LEFT SIDE.
3, J. A. Britton	Wave Crest—H. J. Priest
4, F. Bates	Kosikot—E. V. Atkinson
5, F. P. Farrow	Wendycot—E. V. Atkinson
6, Miss A. Sawyer	Sandycot— Vacant
7, A. Carver	Seaville—Mrs. Petchey
8, C. Brown	Sea Cot—C. Wright
9, H. W. Candler	Theydon Lodge—C. Swan
10, G. W. Osborne	Dungloe—J. Allen

The Frinton directory showing Emma's address.

The 1911 census showing Herbert at Aldershot with other members of the 19th Hussars.

Name:	**Herbert George Columbine**
Age in 1911:	19
Estimated Birth Year:	abt 1892
Birth Place:	Chelsea, London, England
Civil parish:	Aldershot
County/Island:	Surrey
Country:	England
Street Address:	1St Cavalry Brigade, 19Th Hussars, Wellington Lines, Aldershot
Marital Status:	Single
Military unit:	19th Hussars
Registration district:	Farnham
Registration District Number:	34
Sub-registration district:	Aldershot
ED, institution, or vessel:	13
Piece:	3122

Household Members: Name	Age
Albert Thomas Baker	19
Albert William Barber	24
Charles James Baker	21
Albert Francis Barnes	27
Harry Biddel	22
Herry John Bird	19
Robert Charles Boardman	25
Joseph Henry Boon	23
Frank Haveside Bristow	19
Henry Arthur Brimmell	21
John Burnham	22
John Philip Buttress	25
Frank Carnell	29
Arthur Thomas Carter	20
Albert Renal Chapman	22
Reginald George Chapman	20
Charles Clarke	21
William Henry Cleaver	20
William Charles Coe	19
Lionel Coulbourne	19
Herbert George Columbine	19
William Colvin	20
Joseph Cook	19

winter gales of more than 60mph in March. April was no better with over five inches of snow covering the ground on the fifth and day time temperatures failing to rise more than two degrees above freezing. But summer was on its way and May was a lot warmer with only half the average rainfall. As Walton prepared to greet its summer visitors the temperature rose considerably and by July there was over ten hours of sunshine every day and the temperature had risen to 90f. August continued in the same vein with even higher temperatures precipitating a mass exodus to the coast. So many people arrived in Walton that there was not enough accommodation and they had to be turned away. Some even slept in bathing machines while others slept in haylofts with cotton wool in their ears to keep out the beetles.

In the same year the National Insurance Act was introduced to ensure workers received sickness benefit of 9s, free medical treatment and maternity benefit of 30s. For this workers contributed 4d a week, the employer paid 3d and the state 2d. Unemployment benefits were applied much less freely and initially only applied to about two and a quarter million men in seven trades; those in building, iron and steel and ship building. During the war the number of trades covered would grow, as would the number of people covered.

In 1912 free medical treatment for children was introduced followed in 1914 by the introduction of free school meals, but as none of these applied to Emma money was probably always tight.

Emma had enjoyed the past five years living in the fresh air and freedom of Walton, but her peace had been shattered when Bertie had dropped his bombshell earlier in the year. Having never lost his desire to join the army, at the age of seventeen he had caught the train into Colchester and joined up. He was now about to move to Aldershot, the current home of the 19th Hussars. Although there was no war at the moment Emma couldn't stop the feeling of dread that coursed through her body when he had told her what he'd done. It was the same feeling she'd had all those years ago when she'd finished reading his father's last letter.

Chapter 6

3780 Private, Machine Gun Detachment 19th (Queen Alexandra's Own Royal) Hussars

Army life was nothing like Bert had expected and it took him some time to adjust to the strict discipline and rules. But by the time war broke out in 1914 he had settled in and had trouble remembering what life was like before he had signed up.

Before the army had accepted him he'd had to pass several physical tests and be willing to sign on for several years. The conditions varied from regiment to regiment but were normally between five and seven years full time service followed by another five to seven years as a reserve. He had to be aged between eighteen and thirty-eight to be a trooper and be at least five feet three inches tall. He could join up at one of the recruiting offices or at the regimental depot and he would be able to choose which regiment he joined. Those joining the regimental bands could start at fourteen or fifteen and would be paid two shillings a week.

As a recruit he would have lined up in the quartermaster's stores and collected his kit starting with a kit bag, a braided tunic, long overalls with double yellow stripes and a coarse linen bag for his busby. Following this he would have been given a holdall containing a complete shaving kit, a toothbrush, knife, fork and spoon, three greybacks, two khaki tunics, two pairs of khaki slacks, one greatcoat, busby, grenade, plume, lines complete with busby bag, three pairs of socks, three pairs of pants (known as drawers), one service cap and one red walking out cap, one pair of jackboots and one pair of Wellington boots made from good leather.

Once in his barrack room he would have been shown how to fold his tunic and greatcoat properly as well as how to rub raw potatoes over his boots before applying blacking. He would learn how to use his toothbrush handle to improve the shine on his boots and his chin strap and how to sew a button on, mend a sock and repair rips and tears in his trousers.

The army had learned quite a lot from the mistakes made in the Boer War and training had improved considerably. Bertie would first have learnt the basics of drilling, marching, physical fitness, general discipline and essential field craft. Once he had passed through basic training he would have specialized. His training would then be tailored to his role which could be as a rifleman, machine gunner, signaller, bomber or rifle grenadier. Bertie specialized in machine guns and much of his future training was on the use of the Maxim. He would also receive basic training in First Aid, how to set and destroy wire entanglements and as the war came closer this would have included how to deal with gas attacks. The idea was to teach soldiers individual as well as unit discipline, how to follow commands and how to handle weapons safely.

A cavalry regiment consisted of a regimental headquarters, three squadrons and a machine gun section. The machine gun section was under the command of a lieutenant, and had a sergeant, corporal and fourteen privates in the gun teams plus eight men as drivers and two as batmen. These men were trained in the maintenance, transport, loading and firing of the heavy machine gun. These men made up two six-man gun teams, armed initially with the Maxim pattern gun, which was soon replaced by the Vickers. The guns had to have specially designed packs and harnesses made to go with the horses to carry them into battle. Each regiment had a detachment at its base depot, which did not take the field when the regiment was on active service. The base detachment consisted – in theory – of a subaltern, two sergeants and forty-six privates to form a first reinforcement (to make good regimental casualties or other losses); three store-men and the sergeant master tailor.

It was not immediately clear why Bert decided to join the 19th Hussars as there was not an obvious connection to his father's regiment. However the 19th Hussars had been frequent visitors to East Anglia over the preceding years. When the main regiment had been based in Norwich in 1888 it was documented that they had also had a squadron based in Colchester so it may be that when they were again based in Norwich in 1910 one squadron was based in Colchester. Although there would have been other squadrons based there the 19th Hussars had an extremely elegant uniform, blue with gold braid and a white busby-bag, which was very popular with the ladies!

During peace time regiments were always moved around or rotated when troops arrived home from abroad. This also happened when garrisons had extra space and when it was time for a particular regiment to undertake ceremonial duty in London. In garrison towns like Colchester and York the troops stationed there were also rotated. The cavalry would move from town to town on horseback with the non mounted troops travelling by railway. In April 1888 the 19th Hussars had left Norwich and were route marched via Colchester to their new barracks at Hounslow, Hampton Court and Kensington. Here they performed several ceremonial duties. Within three years they were on the move again and in 1891 they arrived in Bangalore in India. From here they moved to Secunderland (India) in 1896 where they remained until posted to Ladysmith in South Africa in 1899. They were based here when the Boer War broke out on 11 October 1899.

Re-designated in 1902 as the 19th (Alexandra, Princess of Wales's Own) Hussars, they were posted to Curragh in Ireland in 1903. After five years they returned to Norwich where they remained until 1910 and then they moved down to Aldershot. Bert was registered on the 1911 census as living in Wellington Lines, Aldershot.

Having just joined up Bert was delighted to arrive at the relatively new, brick built barracks that had replaced the wooden huts. Wellington Lines was the original permanent barracks. It had been built between 1856 and 1859 and renamed after the Duke of Wellington in 1891. There were three cavalry barracks specifically built to house the 1st Cavalry Brigade: Beaumont Barracks was originally known as the South Cavalry Barracks, but was renamed in 1909 to Beaumont after a battle in the Napoleonic Wars with France on 26 April 1794. There was a guardroom and cells, an officers' mess, a sergeants' mess, a riding school plus four, two-storey troop stables, and accommodation for the other ranks which consisted of seventeen men to a room. Warburg Barracks was renamed in 1909 after the battle of Warburg that took place on the 31 July 1760 during the Seven Year's War with France. Before that it had been known as East Cavalry Barracks. It too consisted of a guard room, cells, four two-storey stables, riding school and an officers' and a sergeants' mess. The third cavalry barracks was Willems, renamed from West Cavalry Barracks in 1909 after the cavalry victory in May 1794 during the French Revolutionary Wars. It was laid out in the same way as the others and consisted of a riding school, four two-storey stables, officers' and sergeants' messes and a guard room and cells.

The day started with the trumpeter blowing the cavalry reveille, a long drawn out early morning call, in contrast to the short sharp call of the infantry bugler in Salamanca Lines. Once the men were shaved and dressed, with polished boots and buttons, their beds tidy and the rooms swept, they put on cardigans and tunics, roll puttees and spurs and headed towards the stables. Here they mucked out and groomed the horses and then trotted the horses down the country lanes, each man riding one horse and leading another. Discipline was strict but there was considerable esprit de corps between the men and their officers, even if some of those officers lacked military genius, recruited as they were from the county families who ran the shires.

Once back in the camp the men were taught to ride by the rough-riding sergeant in the riding school. Once considered proficient they were taught the finer arts of sword drill, first from 'imaginary horses' and then the real thing. But it was not all time spent outside as they were also expected to pass the Army First-Class Certificate of Education. Bert was initially surprised there was so much emphasis on knowledge of the Franco-German frontier and very little else. But although nothing was specifically stated it seemed that those in charge considered war with Germany inevitable. Most of their training was intended to make them ready to fight Germany and even in the married quarters the children were now playing games of English versus German.

Although they were trained to use a sword there was more training on the rifle and Maxim machine gun and they also learnt about the German Hotchkiss which was completely automatic and used its own gases to load and fire at the rate of 500-600 rounds a minute. Although horses played a large part in their training on manoeuvres, much of the time was also spent crawling across the ground on their stomachs with rifles.

All sorts of businesses were carried on in the barracks. A 'fruit wallah' brought fruit into the barracks every lunch time and a photographer came in twice a week to take pictures of the soldiers they could send home to their families and sweethearts. A man selling cheap jewellery came round on Saturday nights and a 'tally' man would come round selling clothes on an instalment plan, a 'civvie' suit for five shillings down and the balance to be paid at one shilling a week thereafter. The men initially called this the 'never never' plan until the tally man threatened to go to the CO to report troopers who owed him money. After that payment was made regularly.

As there were few laundry facilities soldiers would often pay someone in the married quarters to wash their whole weeks' laundry for the princely sum of sixpence. Tattoos were quite popular and the tattoo man would charge half a crown for a small regimental crest and five shillings for one with the numbers of the regiment in a floral wreath beneath the crest. Names and tattoos of women were also popular, although when they compared the women afterwards most looked remarkably similar, with their long black hair and full red lips!

The town had several shops that catered entirely to soldiers, from spurs and riding whips, to silk handkerchiefs with the regimental crest in the corner for their girlfriends. Other shops sold regimental badges and Christmas and Easter cards with words like 'To my mother from her soldier son'.

Another place in frequent use in most garrison towns was the 'pox hospital'. Despite lectures and warnings from officers and even the Chaplain-General about the dangers of consorting with 'bad' women, the men paid little heed and many ended up in hospital.

The winter of 1911/12 was extremely bad and several people died from the cold and the freezing conditions. Training was difficult as the lanes were blocked with snow and everything froze for days on end. Civil unrest which had begun earlier in 1911 continued and there were also transport strikes and dock strikes. On 1 March 1912 the suffragettes smashed windows in London's West End and on 15 March a minimum wage for miners was finally introduced after a national strike. On the 11 April the Irish Home Rule Bill was introduced into the Commons, but failed to win the support of the House of Lords. But the real headline news that spring was the sinking of the *Titanic* on its maiden voyage on 15 April with a loss of 1,513 passengers and crew. It was while the world contemplated the horror of the *Titanic* that Bert and the rest of the 19th undertook the move to Hounslow Barracks.

Here they did considerable training on Hounslow Heath, pounding across the Heath on their horses imagining they were in some famous battle in their illustrious regimental past. At times they would pass regiments of marching infantry, their ribald comments about 'bloody horse marines' making them laugh. They had always looked down on the 'toweys', albeit in a good natured way and seeing their heavy packs Bert was more than pleased that he was on horseback, and very proud to be a member of 'The Dumpties' or 'Lillywhites'[1] as they were commonly nicknamed.

To start with London seemed very much how Bert remembered it, but he soon realized that although the richer areas remained the same there was also a considerable undercurrent of discontent that was almost palpable on some days. With no concerns about his own employment Bert, like most of the young men in his squadron, paid more attention to the news that Captain Robert Scott had reached the South Pole. Another item that fascinated him and many other young men was the establishment of the Royal Flying Corps on the 13 April.

Once settled into the Hounslow Barracks, the next couple of years were spent training and undertaking several exercises as well as fulfilling ceremonial duties. Harrow was one of the regular destination for field exercises and it was a common sight to see them marching through London on their way to the countryside of Harrow.

1913 began with the House of Lords again rejecting the Irish Home Rule Bill. This was followed a day later on the 31 January by the founding of The Ulster Volunteer Force to fight Irish Home Rule. More importantly for Bert, was the news on the 10 February of the failure of Captain Scott's 1912 polar expedition.

June 1913 began with the death of suffragette Miss Emily Davison who died after she threw herself under the King's horse at the Derby. But for Bert and the 19th Hussars attention was now concentrated on training and later that month they went to Northampton for more extensive field exercises. While they undertook their field training events Europe took one step closer to war as the Austria-Hungarian Empire began to build up their army. In November 1913 they took part in the Lord Mayor's Show. The streets were full of people and the drum horses of the cavalry regiments competed with each other to be the best. The 19th Hussars boasted a set of silver timpani drums and drum banners of heavy silk with the regimental crest and battle honours embroidered in gold. The day was a spectacular success, but Bert had now been in the army for over two years and still he had not been posted overseas. He enjoyed being based in London as there was always something to do, although not always much money to do it with.

His pay was only seven shillings a week and there were often stoppages for new kit, regimental sport's funds, damage to the barracks and various other things. Most of the men aimed to find a local girl[2] they met up with regularly as there was then a chance they could get invited to the girl's house for supper. Billiards, cards and other games also provided amusement as did music halls, theatres and the new picture houses. There were also more dubious pleasures to be had, but otherwise life was one long round of training, exercises and ceremonial duties and he longed to see action.

Chapter 7

The Great War

There were several reasons for the outbreak of the Great War. In 1914, Russia, Germany, Austria-Hungary, France and Britain all controlled large powerful empires and ruled over millions of people all over the world. Even the less important nations like Turkey, Holland, Portugal, Belgium and Italy had colonies. Having a colony provided a country with status as well as cheap materials for its industry, food and a guaranteed market to export goods to.

Of all the nations Britain's empire was the largest and covered a quarter of the world. France had the second largest empire and there was considerable rivalry between the two countries. In the scramble for Africa, Britain had won the most profitable areas, leaving France and Italy with the Sahara desert and Germany with only a few unimportant colonies.

Germany was a comparatively new country. Until 1870 it had been a collection of independent German speaking states and kingdoms. Now they were one country they were building up their industries as well as their armed forces and were intent on increasing their own empire. There was considerable bitterness in Germany that they were too late to acquire much of an empire as they had started too late.

Unable to build up their own empire Germany decided to become a powerful trading nation instead. Although most countries controlled the trade of their colonies there were still opportunities where they could compete. In South America there were fortunes to be made building railways, factories and harbours. China offered a massive market in which to sell their goods. Although most nations were involved in some rivalry over trade the most contentious appeared to be between Britain and Germany.

Both Japan and Turkey wanted to modernize their armed forces. This meant re-equipping their troops and building ships and although Britain won some contracts it was Germany who did best here. This led to more tension as the Germans won a contract to build a railway that ran right through the Turkish empire to Baghdad. The intention was to link it to the railway that already ran from Berlin through the Austria-Hungarian empire and Bulgaria to Turkey. It soon became known as the Berlin-Baghdad railway and was seen in Britain as a threat to the British owned oilfields in Persia. Rumours even began circulating that it was a jumping off point for an attack on India. These things caused considerable tensions between the European powers, but much more serious was the naval arms race.

Britain had been the biggest naval power since Nelson's defeat of the French and Spanish ships in 1805 at Trafalgar. The Royal Navy protected the merchant fleet all round the world. The Germans began with quite a small warship building programme in 1873 but in 1895 they opened the Kiel Canal. This gave their Baltic ports quick access to the North Sea. Britain saw this as a threat because the German warships were based in these Baltic ports. In 1898 the Germans went even further and built more battleships. By 1905 they had as many warships as France (thirty-six) although Britain still had more with sixty-three. Feeling threatened, the British began to modernize their navy by scrapping obsolete warships and bringing home the overseas fleets so they could be deployed more quickly if necessary. But the biggest threat came when the British launched a new type of warship, HMS *Dreadnought*, in 1906. Its ten- by twelve-inch guns in revolving turrets could fire in any direction without changing course and its shells could carry over eleven miles. It instantly made all the other warships, including new British ones, obsolete, and led to a new phase of the arms race which increased the distrust between the two nations.

Another cause for tension came from the history between France and Prussia which had previously been the most powerful of the German states. In 1870 Prussia had attacked and defeated France and captured their Emperor. At the peace treaty in the Hall of Mirrors at Versailles they had demanded the French give up the two coal and iron rich border states of Alsace and Lorraine. Humiliated, the French were determined to win back their territory so they expanded their army and then stationed most of it along the German border. Germany reacted by doing exactly the same. This left two enormous armies, each comprising thousands of soldiers, facing each other across the border.

On the other side of Europe things were no less tense. Turkey had a large empire consisting of many Russian-speaking Slavs who had no say in their own affairs and whose languages, customs and newspapers had been outlawed. Russia began stirring up nationalistic feelings amongst these people as she could see an opportunity to gain prestige at the expense of the Austrians and Turks. Soon the Croats, Czechs and other Slavs began to see the Russians as their friend and protector, even though the Russians had no real interest in them. Not realizing they were being used these minorities began to demand their freedom, and the Austrians and Turks blamed the Russians for raising the tension between them.

Gradually two armed camps formed. In 1879 feeling isolated Germany formed an alliance with the Austrian-Hungarian Empire which agreed that each would come to the others aid in the event of a war. In 1882 Italy joined them creating a Triple Alliance. Everything was fine until in 1894 France formed a similar alliance with its former enemy Russia. Britain disliked France and Russia almost as much as she disliked Germany, but she began to see the need for allies so in 1902 she signed an alliance with Japan.

As early as 1902 Lt Col William Robertson[1], head of the foreign section of military intelligence, had questioned Britain's treaty obligations to Belgium in the event of a breach of that country's neutrality by either France or Germany. Aware of the growing antagonism in Europe he had suggested that Germany should be regarded as an enemy rather than an ally.

Although his warning was noted in government circles it was still France that was considered to be the natural enemy. However in 1904 Britain and France settled their disagreements and signed the Entente Cordial which was not an agreement to go to war in defence of each other, but gave them both confidence against the ever growing power of the Germans. This was followed in 1907 with a similar agreement with Russia. Although France and Russia were firm allies and had agreed to come to each other's aid in the event of either being attacked, there was still no commitment from Britain to do the same. However Britain did begin modernizing the army, by improving plans for immediate travel and she also created the Territorial Army.

In 1905 the French were having some problems in Morocco so Kaiser Wilhelm II visited Tangier and offered his support for the Moroccans. The French were furious and at an international conference in Algeciras in

Southern Spain, the USA and Britain condemned Germany for interfering. This humiliated the Kaiser and Germany.

In the east of Europe the situation was also deteriorating. Since 1900 the Bosnians had been fighting a terrorist war to try and gain their own freedom from the Turks. In 1908 the Turks gave up Bosnia, but instead of making them independent Turkey handed over control to Austria. The Bosnians appealed to Russia for help, but the Russians looked the other way. Having been defeated only three years earlier by Japan and knowing the Austrians were supported by the Germans, they were not ready yet for another fight.

Things continued to deteriorate between the western Europeans when the German warship *Panther* appeared in Agadir in 1911. Having not forgotten the earlier incident the French were again furious, but this time the British were also worried as they thought the Germans wanted to establish a naval base at Agadir which was close to the vital British naval base in Gibraltar. This time the British threatened war if the Germans did not pull out. Again the Germans were humiliated as they gave way for the second time.

The final straw was the assignation of Arch Duke Ferdinand of Austria in Bosnia in June 1914. Trouble had continued to rumble on in Bosnia with more than a little help from Serbia who provided arms and training for the Bosnian freedom fighters. Although several Austrian diplomats had been killed by assassins the Arch Duke decided he wanted to visit Bosnia and hold a royal procession. At 10.45am Gavrilo Pricip shot both the Arch Duke and his wife Sophia.

Less than a month later the Austrian government sent the Serbian government an ultimatum with ten demands. Although the Serbs agreed to eight of these they could not agree to having Austrian officers in their army or Austrian minsters in their government. So Austria declared war and on the 29 July attacked Serbia. Serbia begged Russia for help and the Russians, who had been waiting for just such an opportunity, headed towards the German and Austrian borders. On the 1 August Germany declared war on Russia and France prepared for war. By the 2 August German troops had moved up to the French and Belgium borders and on the third Germany declared war on France. Britain warned the Germans not to invade Belgium but on the 4 August their troops rolled across the border. Britain immediately declared war on Germany and the horrors of the Great War began.

Chapter 8

Off to War

By July 1914 events in Europe had reached a crisis, but for the 19th Hussars, back in London, training continued as before, as did their recreational activities. The weather was hot and in July they went to Dorney Court on the River Thames to swim the horses.

On the 1 August the papers reported that Germany had declared war. A day later on a quiet afternoon the men were suddenly called up for a general parade. This was most unusual and a sense of urgency ricocheted round the barracks. The men quickly formed up into sections of four in squadron order and marched to their squadron markers. They were joined by the regimental band, also marching to their marker, but to the men's surprise, they were without their instruments.

From the centre door of the officers' mess the colonel emerged. He was closely followed by the second-in-command and the orderly officer. As the sound of the bugle faded into silence the colonel called the regiment to attention. Afterwards Bert could remember nothing other than the final few words '…I am sure you will be a credit to the regiment to which we are all proud to belong' and then the barracks erupted in a surge of delight as the men broke ranks, threw their caps in the air and began slapping each other on the back. The celebrations had begun. Britain was at war and Bert's wish had come true.

They remained in Hounslow until the outbreak of war on 4 August 1914 as the regiment made ready to go to war. After the initial excitement had worn off activity increased in the barracks as swords were taken to the armourers for attention and ammunition boxes and bandoliers were collected, moved and stacked ready for the impending deployment. The limbering wagons and watering carts were checked and everywhere the imaginations of the men were filled with visions of dramatic cavalry charges, amazing victories and incredible heroics.

At night, as the sun went down and the summer sky filled with stars, scores of men crowded round the piano singing the war songs that were fast becoming popular everywhere in the country. *Goodbye Dolly Gray* and *It's a Long Way to Tipperary* were the current favourites and the men sang them with gusto. It was several years since the Boer War and the horrors and privations were seemingly forgotten as preparations gathered pace. Everywhere they looked there were stacks of equipment piling up around the barracks. There was little time now to think about what was to come as their days were filled with parades, inspections, visits to the MO for vaccinations and inoculations, roll calls and more inspections. As the impending departure drew closer evenings became a time for reflection as the men wrote letters home and those who were not writing lay silently on their bunks, lost in their thoughts wondering what was to come.

Just before their departure the regiment was split into divisional cavalry and the men suddenly realized that over a very short time they had been transformed into a mobilized unit. They were now a deadly war machine, their ammunition was live, their equipment was packed away and they were almost ready to leave. It wasn't just inside the barracks that these changes could be seen. On the rare occasion they were allowed out of the barracks they found that the attitude of the civilians towards them had changed completely. From seeing them as drunken, uneducated, promiscuous, redcoats they had suddenly become heroes with everyone wanting to buy them drinks and food and offering them tickets to music halls and theatres. The men took this change of attitude in their stride, albeit with a certain amount of amusement.

As the time for departure grew close parades and inspections grew. One morning, as the men were eating a hearty breakfast of bacon, sausages, bread and butter and hot steaming mugs of tea, rumours started that General Sir John French was coming to inspect the troops. But it turned out to be just a rumour as the parade and inspection was for some officers. By now rumours had also reached the men that they were likely to be outnumbered ten to one by the Germans and a sense of uneasiness had begun to pervade the ranks.

Any conversations inevitably led to a discussion as to where they were going and whether they would find themselves fighting flying machines from their horses. The older, more experienced, South African veterans suggested that at least this time they would know where the enemy was, instead of spending days looking for them as they had done in South Africa. The prevailing view continued to be that victory would be easy and the whole thing would be over before Christmas with the BEF in Berlin celebrating.

But they were also becoming impatient to leave so when they were finally officially informed that they were to move off to go overseas there was pandemonium as the men celebrated. All normal rules were forgotten as the men held 'open house' on the green and in the canteen. In the troop rooms half drunken men danced with women, other men were entwined with women on the narrow iron bunks as they made the most of their last night. The air was filled with the sound of drunken voices singing, as chorus after chorus of the most popular songs were sung. Eventually Last Post echoed across the square only to be drowned out by a particularly loud chorus of *Nellie Dean* and still the alcohol flowed as they partied on. Eventually the bugle signalled 'Lights Out' and by midnight the green and square were finally cleared. At last the men fell into their beds, drunk and exhausted. But for many the silence and darkness sobered them and as they lay on their beds, alone with their thoughts, many found it hard to sleep. The walls of the barracks were now bare, their pictures, postcards and other mementos had been taken down and the euphoria of the past few hours was gradually fading as they wondered what the future held.

The Cavalry Division (later renamed 1st Cavalry Division after the creation of 2nd Cavalry Division on the 16 September 1914) was part of the original British Expeditionary Force which went to France in August 1914.

'A' Squadron went to France with 5th Division and 'B' Squadron with 4th Division. 4th Division were held back briefly to prepare for an invasion by the Germans but were sent to France in time to support the 5th Division in the Battle of Cateau. They were followed in September by 'C' Squadron attached to the 6th Division. 6th Division was a peacetime division and they were not fully equipped and trained until September. They arrived at St Nazaire and went to the Western Front where they remained for the whole war. They arrived just in time to support the BEF at Aisne before the whole army was moved to Flanders.

The full strength of a British cavalry regiment in 1914 was twenty-six officers and 523 other ranks. It consisted of an HQ, machine gun section and three squadrons lettered 'A', 'B' and 'C'. Each squadron had 162 officers and men and was organized into four troops. Each troop of thirty-eight NCOs and troopers was led by subaltern. There were also attached personnel – an armourer sergeant, a corporal and two privates for water duties (RAMC). A British infantry division consisted of 18,073 men of all ranks, 5,592 horses, seventy-six guns and twenty-four machine guns.

On the morning of departure from Hounslow Bert stood stiffly to attention in the square as the colonel addressed the regiment. Every eye was on the colonel, although only the men in the front could really hear what he was saying, as the horses stamping and brasses jangling constantly interrupted the speech. But most were able to piece together enough to hear that they were now off to war, of his pride in taking them there and his confidence in their ability to acquit themselves in keeping with the best traditions of the regiment. He finished by explaining they would be working for the King and country and that if they had to leave some of their comrades on the field of battle that would be the fortune of war and the will of God. As he finished the men cheered for the colonel and then the officers, then for the King and the country.

'A' Squadron then led off and the men rode out of the barracks to the gentle rattling of sword scabbards and rifle buckets, the chinking of spurs and jingling of brasses. There was no pomp or ceremony and only the married women and children were waiting at the gate to see them off. Further down the road a small crowd lining the street cheered 'Three cheers for the Hussars! Three cheers for the Old Mob!' As they marched on the sight of the villages with their rose and ivy covered cottages, the occasional lawns with flagpole and flags flying, and the people bidding them God speed, etched themselves on Bert's memory and he wondered how long it would be before he was back home.

Embarkation to France took place between the 6 and 10 August 1914. Eighteen thousand special trains were laid on over the five days and on the busiest day eight trains ran to Southampton docks. The men were not meant to know where they were going, but having passed through the first few stations out of London it was fairly obvious. And as they swept through the stations one man was heard to say loudly that it was the third time they had passed through 'Bovril'!

On arrival the men let the horses out of the horse boxes gingerly and the smell of horses mingled with the sharp tangy smell of the sea. The long drawn out sounds from the ship's sirens mixed with the short blasts of the rapidly arriving and departing trains, the horns from motor vehicles and even the odd gramophone. While the horses were fed the men were given hot mugs of tea to drink with their rations, and in the background a band played popular tunes. Once fed the men and horses were ready to head towards the quay leaving behind numerous woodbine cigarette ends, spent matches and horse manure.

Eighty thousand troops, 30,000 horses, 315 field guns and 125 machine guns were now assembled at Southampton and Portsmouth. Transport and supplies were mainly sent from Avonmouth and Liverpool. On the 9 August the ships began to depart at ten minute intervals with an average of thirteen ships leaving each day. As each ship left the dock every other ship in the harbour blew its whistles and horns and all the men on the decks cheered. Advance parties had already gone to Rouen, Boulogne and Havre to prepare the camping grounds and assembly points for the main body.

The Royal Navy was confident that it had sealed the Channel from any attack so the ships departed at night without escorts. The Royal Navy was not in evidence because the Grand Fleet based in the Orkneys had contained the main German forces in their harbours. The Channel Fleet, Harwich Force and French Channel Flotillas had also completely blocked the Channel to German light forces.

The ship looked enormous, its shape silhouetted against the evening sky. The men and horses climbed the long gangplank. It was slatted to make it easier for the horses but some still hesitated at the steep incline and had to be encouraged. Having settled the horses the men loosened their tunic collars, took off their puttees and rewound them more loosely and, out of habit, began checking their rifles. While some sat down by the engine room Bert went up on deck to get some fresh air. As they set off across the English Channel to France he wondered what his father had been thinking of, as he too watched the coastline of England recede into the distance. Although it was dark it was cloudless, the moon was shining brightly and the sky was filled with thousands of stars. Like so many other men on the ships Bert had never been abroad and he could hardly contain his excitement. The decks were overcrowded with men and equipment and even though it was calm several men felt seasick. Bert smiled as he suddenly remembered his father's letter to his mother talking of how the men had been so seasick they couldn't leave their hammocks.

Fortunately he was like his father and felt perfectly well, so while others tried to get some sleep he remained upright and gazed out at the vast open space of the English Channel and the convoy of ships following them to France.

Eventually lulled into exhaustion by the gently lapping waves rhythmically slapping against the side of the ship he decided he had better get some sleep or he would be really tired when they arrived. Carefully settling down on the overcrowded deck, taking care not to wake those already asleep, he closed his eyes and tried to stem his rising excitement. He had waited so long to be sent anywhere and now there was a war he was going to be right in the thick of it. He finally drifted off into a deep sleep, his dreams filled with heroic deeds and anticipation as to what the next few weeks would bring.

It was probably the sudden lack of engine noise that woke him. He opened his eyes and found himself gazing up at an inky black sky filled with thousands of dancing stars all twinkling down on him. The night was still warm and the moon was shining brightly, illuminating everything for miles around. He sat up cautiously so as not to wake anyone else and peered cautiously out into the moonlit channel.

The sea was completely calm, the waves barely rippling the surface and all he could see were transport ships stretching into the distance as far as the eye could see. There were no destroyers or other protective vessels in sight, they were all alone. Bert sat mesmerized, gazing out across the water until he realized that he was not the only person awake. A little further along the crowded deck another soldier was also gazing enthralled at the enormous convoy on its way to France. Seeing Bert's quizzical look he quickly pointed out that they were probably waiting for the transports from the other embarkation ports to rendezvous with them mid channel. Bert nodded and resumed watching and before long he heard the unmistakable sound of ship's engines. They watched silently as the other transport ships arrived and then the engines restarted and they were again on their way to the Continent.

The main disembarkation ports were Rouen, Boulogne and Havre. At all the ports the troops of the BEF were greeted with wild enthusiasm and in Havre the French Garrison even climbed on the roof of their barracks and cheered as they watched their allies coming down the ships gang planks in the blazing August sun. The area was full of French soldiers in their various blues and reds, their officers identifiable by their high box caps, the infantry men, their rifles held awkwardly, marching out of step and reminding Bert of his days in training.

Once they had all disembarked the arduous business of entraining them for the front line began. The railways in France were under the control of the French who had different operating procedures than those in Britain. In Britain an infantry battalion would be carried on two medium-sized trains at 25mph whilst the French preferred one long train travelling at 12mph. This would cause considerable disruption in the future, especially when the Germans overran some of the important rail centres such as Amiens. To overcome these problems thirty British officers were installed to liaise with the French railway authorities under an Inspector General of Communication and things began to improve. In November 1914 control of the railways was moved to the Quarter Master General who was already in control of troop movements at GHQ. The Supply Directorate also moved there in 1915.

To Bert it seemed to have taken forever to get all the men on board with their equipment. For the men who boarded first there was now a long, hot, uncomfortable wait as the rest entrained. The train became more and more overcrowded and despite the open windows there was little air. Bert soon gave up looking out the window and sank to the floor with the others fervently wishing they would just start so that at least there would be some air circulating through the overcrowded train. Eventually, with everyone safely aboard the train, it began to move slowly out of the station. Twelve miles an hour was not very fast and was not quick enough to circulate any air so the temperature remained unbearable hot. After a few miles at the same pace jokes began to circulate amongst the men about being able to march quicker and at least outside the train they would be cooler.

Hot, bad tempered and extremely fed up they finally arrived in Amiens on 14 August. Here, much to their relief, they were able to detrain for the long advance to the concentration areas around Le Cateau and Maubeuge. As the men breathed in the fresh air, lined up and prepared to march, they were blissfully unaware that General Alexander von Kluck's German Army of 160,000 men had begun moving down from Liege, putting them on a collision course with the BEF.

Once off the overcrowded cramped conditions of the train their spirits began to rise and they began to take an interest in their surroundings. The road appeared to stretch out in front of them for miles, far straighter than any road Bert had ever seen. Behind and in front of them were masses of troops, transport, guns and staff cars. As at home they marched alternatively at ease and at attention. At regular intervals they dismounted and walked before remounting and beginning the process again. As they marched cheerfully along the poplar lined roads to Le Cateau and Mons they were greeted enthusiastically by the local population. The greetings became even more enthusiastic the further north they went. From cries of '*Vivent les Anglais*' they were now kissed, decked out with flowers and offered all kinds of food and drink on tables specially laid out for them for which their offers to pay were cheerfully turned away. Despite Kitchener's dire warning of the need to resist the temptations that might face them from women and drink, in no time members of the BEF had joined in the fun.

Having tossed their regimental badges, caps and belts to the hundreds of smiling girls and other admirers they were soon marching along the roads with tweed peasant caps on their heads and their trousers held up with string. Bert and his two companions, relaxing on their transport cart with their machine gun and ammunition, laughed and joked as their horses pulled them along behind the cheerful marching men. It was a warm sultry day, the sun was shining brightly in a cloudless blue sky and Bert, like the rest of the men, was enjoying himself immensely. There was no sign of the enemy and the adulation from the civilians was very welcome as they headed towards Mons where they would dig in for the night. Ahead, equally ignorant about the advance of the 70,000 British soldiers with their 300 guns, was the German 1st Army with 160,000 men and 600 guns.

Chapter 9

Mons

The 1st and 2nd German Armies were the right wing of the Shlieffen Plan. It was intended that they would sweep eastwards from the channel ports to envelope Paris driving the French armies back onto their own defences. Having brought the Western Front to a rapid conclusion, they could then turn their attention and resources to the eastern front. Sir John French, the commander of the BEF, had been expecting to join a French offensive into Belgium, but this plan had been based on the wrong information about the German plan. The retreat of the French 3rd and 4th Armies from the German 1st and 2nd Armies had left the French 5th Army exposed on its right flank, and on the 22 August the French had suffered a serious setback at the Sambre, when their 5th Army had been attacked by the German 2nd and 3rd Armies.

That night, in order to give the French armies time to reorganize, the BEF was ordered to launch a counter attack at what was mistakenly believed to be the right flank of the German Army advancing through Belgium. Fortunately French ignored the request, as the German 1st Army under General von Kluck was heading straight for the British position. Instead he promised to hold the canal for twenty-four hours with I Corps under General Douglas Haig on the British right and II Corps under General Sir Horace Smith-Dorrien on the left.

Although they were considerably outnumbered the British did have an advantage in that many members of the BEF had years of experience gained in the Boer and other colonial wars. They had learned valuable lessons from the Boers who had combined accurate rifle fire with an ability to dig deep trenches. By 1914 the British regular soldier could fire fifteen aimed shots a minute.

On arrival in Mons the infantry took up entrenched positions along twenty miles of the Mons-Conde canal which runs along the northern outskirts of the town. The canal was no more than seven feet deep, had an average width of sixty-four feet and there were eighteen bridges. It ran through a mining area that was lined with houses, mine buildings, spoil heaps, and numerous deep drainage ditches. The slag heaps were invariably overlooked by higher ones and the higher ground had woods and spinneys that fringed the canal and caused problems with visibility and mobility. It was hardly an ideal environment for a defensive battle, but the British dug themselves in as best they could. By the time the Germans reached the canal on 22 August, the British were virtually invisible.

The role of the 19th Hussars here included reconnaissance, providing flank and advance guards and screening and deployment as a mobile reserve. Bert and some of the 5th Division were sent to defend the middle section of the canal while the rest of the 5th Division gradually spread a mile further northwards towards Hautrage which was on the northern side of the canal.

At 5.30am on the morning of the 23 August at his HQ in a chateau in Sars-la-Bruyere, Sir John French met Haig, Allenby and Smith-Dorrien to discuss tactics. Smith-Dorrien had serious concerns about the II Corps' position on the canal. It was no good for a protracted defence as they were trying to defend a twenty-one mile front. Other British positions were also exposed so French ordered the outposts on the canal to be strengthened and the bridges to be demolished. Smith-Dorrien then pointed out that if the outposts came under too much pressure II Corps would evacuate Mons and take up defensive positions among the pit villages and slag heaps further to the south. He left believing that French had agreed.

It was raining and misty as 'A' Squadron 19th Hussars began reconnoitring the area on the morning of the 23 August. It was difficult to see clearly the approaches to the canal from the north because of the houses, factories and slag heaps and they had to be extremely cautious. Bert had been in position all night by his machine gun and was wet through, visibility was poor and the rain was falling relentlessly. In the distance he could hear birds singing and, other than the pattering of the rain, everything seemed quiet and peaceful.

Wishing he could get up and stretch Bert began wondering how long he had to wait before he would be relieved, when suddenly the air was filled with the sound of guns. The German cavalry had begun firing on the British infantry outposts at Obourg, Nimy and Ville Pommeroeul and a desperate fire fight was now underway. Initially the Germans attacked in a piecemeal fashion and were reasonably easy to contain, but then they began to attack in a more organized way. Although the infantry tried hard to hold onto their outposts while the main infantry battalions took up their positions, they were unable to because of the sheer weight of the attack.

By 9am the Germans had gained the high ground on the canal and had opened fire on the main positions of the 4th Middlesex and 4th Royal Fusiliers. It was now the turn of the artillery, and the bombardment that followed was terrifying. Shells landed all around the defenders blowing massive holes in the ground. They became increasingly more accurate helped by a German spotter plane which circled lazily above pointing out their positions to the gunners. As the artillery stopped abruptly the German infantry began to advance. The attacks gained in intensity and ferocity as units of IX Korps began attacking from across the other side of the canal from Obourg to Nimy. Wave after wave of German infantry now advanced towards the British defenders, their dense grey lines seemingly unending as they ploughed forward, regardless of the increasing numbers of casualties. Dead and wounded littered the battlefield, their corpses adding more obstacles to the advancing Germans. But still they kept coming, shoulder to shoulder, each battalion still advancing in three double ranks. The British held their nerve, their rifle fire so rapid and accurate that many Germans believed they were facing massed machine guns.

The British infantry man was using the Lee-Enfield III rifle which had a muzzle velocity of 734 yards per minute. They were able to fire from a prone position and to fire fifteen rounds a minute accurately. As the Germans advanced in massed formation they cut them to pieces, each bullet often taking out two men because of their close proximity to each other.

Bert had no time to be frightened, no time to take in the mass of enemy forces bearing down on them. Aiming carefully he concentrated on firing his machine gun, a Maxim which had a maximum rate of fire of 500 rounds per minute, the equivalent of forty well-trained riflemen. He was intent on bringing down as many as possible before they could cross the canal and overrun them. As the battle raged on he lost track of time, thirst, heat, fear, everything forgotten in the adrenaline of the moment.

The fighting continued unabated as the men put up a stubborn resistance and prevented the Germans from crossing over the canal. Eventually one

German managed to jump into the canal despite the intense British fire and was able to close the swing bridge before being killed. This act of heroism by Private Niemeyer enabled the first Germans to cross the canal, but still the fighting continued.

The battle now seemed to be raging all round Bert. The air was filled with the screams of the wounded and dying, the tap tap tap of rapid rifle fire and staccato bursts from the other machine gun which echoed his. Both machine guns were served by a section of twelve men and one subaltern. However, many of those had now been killed or wounded, and after a while Bert found himself alone. The rain had long since ceased falling and the sun was now beating down mercilessly. The machine gun was getting hot and he had very little water left with which to cool it. Acrid smoke was wafting aimlessly in the hot, still, morning air reducing visibility, clogging his eyes and nose and making it hard to breathe. His head was beginning to hurt and his throat was dry, his tongue swollen from the heat and dehydration. Dirt, stones and coal slag blown into the air by the constant shelling were landing indiscriminately on both sides causing more casualties and adding to the chaos and confusion that surrounded him.

The day wore on and the fighting continued yet somehow, despite being heavily outnumbered, the men held their positions. As the sun finally went down and the fighting ceased Bert gratefully let go of his machine gun and eased back into his trench. The gun was burning hot from the constant firing and he had to remember not to touch the barrel. For the first time in hours he was able to take a drink from his water bottle and the warm liquid felt like nectar as it slid down his painfully dry throat. He had no water left at all to cool the gun. If they started again before it had cooled down he, or one of the others, would have to urinate on it. He glanced round and saw that those closest to him who had survived were also taking time to drink. There was little banter, just relief they were still alive and that, for the moment anyway, the canal line had been held. The first day's fighting between the BEF and the Germans was over and victory had gone to the British.

With the intention of continuing the fight the following day, that night French ordered the BEF to pull back a short distance to the south and to create a new defensive line. However, the French were still in full retreat to the east and this was opening up a dangerous gap between the BEF and the French 5th Army. French was left with little option but to make the difficult decision to order a general retreat, a retreat that would last for two weeks and cost more casualties than had fallen at Mons itself.

For Bert the first day's fighting had been a mixture of exhilaration and fear. As they loaded up the gun onto the cart and began the withdrawal southwards he wondered what the next day would bring. So far very few of his friends had been killed or wounded but he had seen the carnage on the other side of the canal and had a feeling it was only a matter of time before their own casualty rates rose. He wondered what his mother was doing and whether she knew where he was. For the first time since he'd joined up Bert felt the stirrings of guilt. A vivid picture of his mother's expression when she'd found out about his father came unbidden into his mind. He shook his head angrily to dispel the memory. He had no intention of getting killed. In any case it would all be over by Christmas wouldn't it?

It was not until 11am on 24 August that 5th Division were finally forced to retire. The German III Korps had now joined in the attack at Jemappes which was two miles west of Mons and the front was continuing to spread westwards. The Royal Scots Fusiliers began withdrawing from their position north of the canal while the Germans advanced towards the bridge at Lock 2. Here they were held and pinned down for several hours by the intensity and accuracy of the British fire. Even further west the Brandenburg Grenadiers advanced swiftly to Terte where they too were halted, this time by the numerous British defensive barbed wire entanglements. They soon became bogged down in the ditches and dykes and were unable to advance through the crossfire of the West Kent's and Scottish Borderers who were still positioned on the canal bank and hanging on tenaciously.

By midday on the 24 August there was fighting along the entire length of the straight part of the canal and by mid afternoon the continuous artillery bombardment and infantry attacks had taken their toll on the battalions in the west and they began to fall back. As they fell back their luck ran out. Because of the lack of exploders to fire the charges they failed to blow the bridges near Frameries and this allowed the Germans to cross the canal, perilously close to the Scots Fusiliers who were now in full retreat.

Having passed the canal west of Obourg the Germans had reached the railway station. They had taken heavy casualties whilst advancing in massed formation, but they had quickly learned their lesson and were now advancing in extended order. This advance soon threatened the Middlesex and Irish who found themselves under observation from the high ground on the north of the canal. They were also being threatened from the rear by several advanced Germans patrols pushing through from Mons. Although the Royal Fusiliers had already begun to withdraw from Nimy, the Middlesex and Royal Irish managed to hold on until 3.15pm. Then, having taken over 100 casualties, they began to pull back to Mons. Here they reformed before moving on to Ciply.

With the enemy so close on their heels the withdrawal soon became chaotic. The retreating engineers had only managed to blow up one bridge and they'd had an officer captured at Nimy Bridge. Those who had been ordered to defend until the last man to cover the withdrawal were soon completely over run as the Germans swarmed through Nimy and along the straight road into the city. As there was no planned defence line the withdrawal soon became a rout. Parties of infantry quickly became mixed up and command devolved down to captains and senior NCOs.

After barely three days as divisional cavalry 5th Division had been returned to their more conventional role. As they withdrew they met up with General de Lisle on the 25 August and were then ordered to join the 2nd Cavalry Brigade. Meanwhile 'B' Squadron had arrived at St Quentin. From here they had been marched to the Bois de Gallignies but were unable to meet up with 4th Division. On route they met up 'A' Squadron and the 2nd Cavalry Brigade and were ordered to join them, thus forming a composite regiment with the 4th Dragoon Guards. The 2nd Cavalry Brigade was then used to plug the gap between the 1st and 2nd German armies whilst the rest of the BEF made good their withdrawal along the railway line to Busigny.

The Battle of Mons was over but the retreat had just begun. The British had taken around 1,600 casualties compared to estimated German casualties of between 3,000 and 5,000. However, while Germany could afford to take quite large casualties, Britain's volunteer forces could ill afford to lose 1,600 experienced regulars. By the end of the year the fighting at Mons, Le Cateau and in the First Battle of Ypres came perilously close to annihilating the whole of the pre war British Army. Even more serious was the estimated sixty per cent reduction in fire power strength. Never again would the same consistency and accuracy be available because the casualties were replaced by newly trained conscripts and volunteers and there was simply no time to train them to the degree their predecessors had been trained.

Chapter 10

The Retreat from Mons

As they retreated from Mons they were repeatedly attacked by advance parties of German cavalry and infantry. The sun blazed down mercilessly as they retraced their footsteps through villages that only a few days earlier had greeted then as heroes. Now shutters were closed and the inhabitants, for the most part, had fled westwards to escape the rapidly advancing Germans. With little food and virtually no water the heat began to take its toll on the marching men. Those with the machine guns were slightly better off as they had carts on which to transport them, pulled by horses. The men took it in turns to ride the horses so did not have to march all the way. The British cavalry never rode their horses all the time anyway so many of the officers also walked. But, even for them, the relentless heat and lack of food and water was exhausting. Despite strict orders to the contrary, the roads were littered with abandoned kit as the men threw away their overcoats and items they considered unnecessary, rather than carry them. They were constantly held up by refugees who were also fleeing the fighting. The roads were crammed with adults and children, carts and all manner of vehicles and animals as they too headed westwards, away from the rapidly advancing Germans.

While the retreat continued, General Smith-Dorrien's II Corps came under attack from Von Kluck's 1st Army near Le Cateau. They had arrived at Le Cateau in the early evening of the 25 August during a heavy thunder storm, the men wet, hungry and even more weary thanks to the torrential rain which had drenched them. Smith-Dorrien's three divisions and a small cavalry corps were separated from Haig's 1 Corps which was now eight miles to the east at Landrecies. Realizing that even if he tried to withdraw, he would have been under attack, he made the decision to stand and fight. His troops had been fighting a retreat for the last couple of days and were completely exhausted so tactically, as well as psychologically, he considered it was the sensible thing to do. However, this was against the orders of French, who had ordered a complete withdrawal of all the troops.

On the morning of 26 August II Corps were attacked by six German divisions – three infantry and three cavalry. The British line was along the length of the road between Le Cateau and Cambrai and the German artillery opened up across the eight miles of open ground that was held by Smith-Dorrien's forces and continued unabated until noon when the infantry began to advance towards them. But the British had dug in well and were positioned in shallow trenches in much the same way as they had at Mons. As it had been at Mons the tactic was extremely successful with their fast and accurate rifle fire inflicting heavy losses on the advancing Germans. But when two more German divisions joined the battle, II Corps came close to defeat. Towards the end of the day the German II Korps was approaching from the direction of Cambrai. This meant the British line was in danger of being outflanked at both ends. The threatened envelopment was prevented by the arrival of General Sordet's French Cavalry Corps on the left. This allowed II Corps to withdraw over night and continue their retreat south towards Paris and Marne.

Losses were high on both sides with the British taking between 7,000 and 8,000[1] casualties and losing thirty-eight guns, but it successfully slowed up the German's advance on Paris and also caused several thousand German casualties.

Despite Smith-Dorrien's relative success French was furious, resenting his decision to fight. This led to an extremely acrimonious argument between the two men which eventually led to Smith-Dorrien's retirement on the grounds of ill health the following year. By now French was totally demoralized by the losses at Mons and Le Cateau and feared that the BEF might have to be brought out of the line to recover.

Meanwhile II Corps had joined the rest of the BEF as they headed westwards. The men had been marching non-stop now with little or no food for several days. The further they went the more disorderly the lines became, as regiments became mixed up and discipline broke down. At night they would wait until they arrived at a town and then dig in on the high ground. The few remaining machine guns would do the same. Although the

Germans harried them they did not initially attack in strength, but the constant strain became too much for some. Wishing for nothing more than to go home and not have to fight anymore the sound of rifle fire as men shot themselves in the foot became common.

In St Quentin the situation became even more serious. 5th Division had reached St Quentin by the 27 August. Here they stopped for a couple of hours while they had some food and then continued. But stragglers continued to enter the town together with much larger groups of men who had become separated from their proper formations. This included half a battalion from 4th Division who were miles off course. Behind them came two squadrons under the command of Major Tom Bridges who were the cavalry rearguard. Supporting them were some French Territorials. When he entered St Quentin he was horrified to find men lying around all over the main square. Although he ordered them to stand up and rejoin their units he was ignored. Realizing the danger they were in if a German advance party should arrive he ordered the French to set up outposts round the edge of the town, dig in and prepare to hold through to the afternoon. He then went to find some more senior officers to help pull the exhausted men back into line. Back in St Quentin he found the remains of the battalions. They had piled their weapons up in the railway station when their commanding officers had given their word to the town's Mayor that they would surrender so that the town would not be bombed.

Furious, Bridges removed the document from the Mayor and sent his interpreter to tell the men to fight. The men held a meeting and then informed Bridges that they had already surrendered and had no intention of fighting. Furthermore they would only move from the town if a train was sent to collect them as they were not walking any further. Bridges replied with an ultimatum that he would provide transport for those who genuinely couldn't walk but if the rest were not ready in an hour he would ensure that no British soldiers were left alive in the town when he left.

His next problem was the group of men in the town square who were too worn out to get up. Finding a toy shop he came out with a tin whistle and toy drum and he and his men began marching round the fountain playing marching songs much to the amusement of the exhausted men. At first they just laughed but then, after Bridges promised he would see they got back to their regiments, they fell in.

Having resolved the problem Bridges rode out to where he had ordered the French to set up their outposts, only to find they had gone leaving the town completely undefended.

But as they left St Quentin behind their problems were only just beginning. Fear of the advancing Germans meant that even more refugees had taken to the roads. Their belongings were piled high on carts, bikes, perambulators, trucks, wheelbarrows, even tiny carts drawn by dogs, anything that could carry bedding, clothes and other precious possessions. Alongside them were their cows, goats and horses which only served to add to the chaos and hampered the retreat even more. Most had run out of food and water and were begging for some from the British soldiers who had none to give. Although it was against orders, many of the men dropped out during the march only to reappear later having managed to get lifts on carts and even horses. When they returned they often looked worse than the ones who had continued marching. Water was rationed to only half a pint a day and anyone found drinking native water or stealing food from the abandoned properties was sentenced to field punishments.

The men were tired, unshaven, thirsty and hungry, their feet were sore and still the retreat continued. Every so often they would have to fight against the increasingly bold attacks from the rapidly advancing Germans. From the monotonous weary marching along the roads and tracks they would suddenly find themselves digging into ditches and fighting for their lives. When the fighting finished there was no time to bury the dead, only time to get back out on the road and continue the relentless retreat.

As they left Chauny on the 30 August they found themselves under artillery bombardment yet again and had to withdraw back three miles. As the bombardment finished the German infantry attacked. The attacks were sustained and continued all day. The men held on and appeared to be successfully beating back the Germans, but despite this they were still ordered to retire.

The retreat continued westwards. Behind them the Royal Engineers were busy blowing up bridges after they'd crossed, but still the Germans advanced. The pattern was always the same. First their artillery barrages bombarded them as the Germans sought to find the correct range, followed by mass infantry attacks. Most frustrating and psychologically damaging for the men was that time after time, despite seeming to have the advantage, they were ordered to retire. Then it was back to more endless marching.

By the 31 August, they had been retreating for seven days. Some of the men had resorted to wrapping puttees round their feet instead of wearing boots, others were walking in socks, their feet bleeding profusely as they walked along the rough roads, while the luckier ones had found soft shoes from somewhere. Others were frightened to take their boots off, even though they were falling to pieces and some were walking with blood soaked rags tied round their feet. Those on horses and carts frequently swapped places with those on foot, but it made little difference as by now they were staggering rather than marching, lack of food and rationed water making it almost unbearable to put one foot in front of the other.

There were occasional lighter moments as when someone found a mouth organ and began to play it, the jaunty tunes reviving the weary men for a few moments. But these were few and far between and as they staggered on the men found themselves falling asleep whilst on their feet, causing them to trip up and fall over. The days had now fallen into a familiar pattern as they headed ever westwards. From walking they would find themselves fighting off an attack and then, once that was repelled, back to walking again. Any semblance to marching had long since ceased as only sheer determination was keeping them going. Each step was a miracle of mind over pain and yet still they kept going. Dawn until dark, dark until dawn, fighting, marching, fighting, marching, each day less men answering the roll call as men died or were wounded or just went missing.

On the 1 September the German 1st Army changed direction and instead of heading towards Paris turned towards Chauny. The Germans were now advancing in a south-easterly direction while the BEF was retreating in a south-westerly direction.

I Corps had halted near the northern exit of the Foret de Villers Cotterets and the left of the French 5th Army was twelve miles further north near Vauxaillon. II Corps had reached the Coyolles area which was south-west of the Villers Cotterets and Crepy-en-Valois. Bert and the rest of 5th Division were positioned on the east flank. II Corps was on the south-west of the forest leaving a gap of about five miles between the inner flanks of I Corps and III Corps.

As the German troops advanced, they ran into the rear guard of the BEF at Nery, Crepy-en-Valois and Villers Cotterets. The 1st Cavalry Brigade soon found themselves in serious trouble in Nery when the Germans managed to place ten field guns within 800 yards of their camp. With shells raining down from all sides they were completely pinned down and soon began taking heavy casualties. In desperation they sent a runner to ask for assistance from the 1st Middlesex who set off immediately to help. On arrival they found many dying and wounded men and several dead horses lying in rows. 'D' Company of the 1st Middlesex attacked the German guns with their bayonets and managed to capture eight of them. The German gun crews fled, leaving the guns, two of which were loaded, behind. However, there were no horses left to pull them, so they disabled them by removing the sights and breaking the elevating gear. These were to be the first German guns captured in the Great War.

By the 2 September the relentless sun and the dust from the roads was making life intolerable. There were even more refugees cramming the roads than before, many who appeared to be in a worse condition than they were. The sight of starving children was too much for many of the men and they gave them what was left of their own meagre rations of bully beef (tinned corned beef) and biscuits even though it was obvious that for many it would be too late. The hundreds of refugees weaving and straggling across the road were beginning to pose a severe threat to the retreat as men found themselves separated from each other and unable to get through. Despite their exhaustion the only sensible option was to get back into some semblance of a marching line so they could get past.

For many the worst day was when they came within reach of the River Aisne. With the pursuers rapidly gaining on them they were now forced to march non-stop for several miles to get across before the Royal Engineers blew up all the bridges. With no rest stops, weak and exhausted men dropped like nine pins and were unable to get up again. The remaining soldiers had no option but to march round them as they did not have the strength to lift their feet high enough to climb over them. There was no question of trying to help as they knew that if they bent down to help they too would fall over and be too weak to get up again.

Despite the total, mind numbing, exhaustion that was now their constant companion there was still a need to post sentries when they did stop. Although the army was in full retreat military discipline still prevailed, and at least two men who were found asleep by an officer were court-martialled and shot for falling asleep on duty.

By the 5 September the reserves that had been sent from England finally arrived and joined them. For the clean shaven, tidy and well fed reserves the first sight of the BEF they had come to fight with must have been extremely disheartening. The men and officers who had survived the 251 mile retreat were filthy and had long beards, many with lice infestations. Any equipment they still had was torn, dirty and often lacking vital parts. Their clothes were in tatters, their feet in old shoes, field boots or bandaged in blood soaked rags. Their trousers had been cut to ribbons and the only head coverings were peasant caps, women's hats, virtually anything they could find. As they finally arrived in the concentration area and wearily set up camp they were told that their overcoats could now be discarded which resulted in several derisory cheers from those who had not thrown them away and even more laughter from those who had.

The final casualty figures for the Mons Campaign came to just over 150,000 men and officers killed, wounded and missing and the loss of forty-two guns. Most of the losses were sustained by II Corps.[2]

Chapter 11

The Race to the Coast

By the 6 September the Germans had advanced so rapidly that they were within thirty miles of Paris and the French capital prepared itself for a siege. The BEF and the French had been retreating continuously since 25 August and were exhausted and demoralized and had now reached the River Marne. The German 1st Army was ordered to encircle Paris from the east while the French Government, fearing the imminent collapse of the city, left for Bordeaux.

But the French were determined not to give up their capital without a fight. On the same day, the Commander in Chief of the French Forces, General Joseph Joffe ordered a counter attack. General Maunoury's 6th Army of 150,000 men was sent to attack the right flank of the German 1st Army. In turning to repel the attack the Germans allowed a thirty mile wide gap to appear in the German lines, between the German 1st and 2nd Army. Troops from the BEF joined the French 5th Army as they poured through the gap while simultaneously attacking the German 2nd Army. Despite the success of the counter attack the German forces still came perilously close to breaking through. It was only the arrival of 6,000 reserve infantry troops who were ferried in from Paris by 600 taxi cabs on the 7 September that saved the day and finally turned the battle in favour of the Allies.

On the 8 September the French 5th Army followed up their success by launching a surprise attack against the German 2nd Army which widened the gap between the two German Armies even more. Fearing an Allied breakthrough the Germans began an orderly retreat northwards on the 9 September, pursued by the French and the British, who were now able to cross the River Marne.

However the BEF and the French were totally exhausted after their own rapid retreat and also too cautious to hurry headlong after the retreating Germans. Their pursuit was much too slow, a mere twelve miles on the first day. After forty miles the German 1st Army crossed the River Aisne to the high ground of the Chemin des Dames ridge. Here they stopped at a point north of the River Aisne where they were reunited with 2nd Army and the new 7th Army. Once there they began digging the trenches that were to last for several years.

The Battle of Marne ended on the 10 September and was a strategic triumph for the BEF and the French. They had not only succeeded in beating back the Germans and regaining lost ground, they had also ended any hope the Germans might have had of adhering to the Shlieffen Plan, which needed a swift end to the war on the Western Front so attention and resources could be concentrated on the east.

However, casualties were extremely heavy with the French taking 25,000 and the Germans a similar number. Britain recorded another 12,733 casualties from its experienced regular army, reducing its effectiveness even more.

Having failed to exploit the German retreat by not pursuing them quickly enough, the French 5th and 6th Armies, together with the BEF launched a frontal assault on the now firmly entrenched German positions on the evening of the 12 September. They managed to establish a bridgehead north of the river on the 14 September and used the plateau to continue the assault on the enemy. However, it was not long before the Germans counter attacked, forcing the Allies back. Despite several concerted attempts to take the German position the Allies were unable to consolidate any gains as they were continually driven back by the defensive use of machine guns and heavy artillery. By the 18 September the Allies began scaling back the number of attacks and by the 28 September fighting had ceased altogether. The French were finding themselves under pressure at Reims and both sides realized that the enemy was too well entrenched for their frontal assaults to have any success.

Both forces now attempted to manoeuvre past each other instead. The race to the sea began with the French moving north-west to attack the exposed German right flank at Noyon.

As the British II Corps disembarked from the train at Abbeville on the 8 and 9 October Bert looked round at his new surroundings with interest. The BEF had moved to Flanders for several reasons. One was to be closer to the coast which would aid communications and supply lines of equipment and much needed reserves. It would also allow them to defend the coast much better if needed. Thirdly it would help avoid the communication difficulties caused by the French and British lines crossing each other. However, most of II Corps had no idea where they were, let alone why.

The train journey from the River Aisne had been cramped and uncomfortable but after the dreadful retreat from Mons no one had felt like complaining. At least they weren't walking and it wasn't as hot and stuffy as their first train journey had been back in August.

The platform was soon crowded with disembarking troops all looking as weary as he felt. He had tried to make the most of the inactivity and grab some sleep on the train but it was difficult. Every time he closed his eyes he could hear the booming of the heavy guns and see images he would prefer not to remember.

There had been very little respite since the fighting had begun at the end of August. The retreat had been even more dangerous than the battle with advance parties of Germans attacking them at every opportunity. After the retreat had ended there had been an all too brief taste of victory as they beat the Germans back from Paris and then it had been their turn to pursue the Germans. But their triumph had not lasted long and soon they found themselves pinned down on the River Aisne by ever increasing artillery bombardments and fierce machine gun fire.

'A' Squadron had finally rejoined 5th Division on the 15 September and as one of the few remaining machine gunners Bert found himself becoming one of the main targets for the unpleasantly accurate German artillery. Being either positioned on the front line, usually at a prominent corner to cover a salient or in a saphead[1] so he could cover the line with enfilade fire, made him a very conspicuous target.

Even worse, as the infantry ducked into the safety of the trenches, he had to keep his head out so he could see what he was firing at, not to mention sighting and loading the gun. Having survived Mons he had thought that he knew what to expect. But the artillery at Mons was nothing like the bombardment they had been subject to at Aisne and even now he shuddered as he remembered the shock they had received.

On arrival two of his companions had dug in while he and the remaining men had unpacked the gun, tripod and ammunition. The gun was placed in the trench, they checked the arc of fire and then set about camouflaging the position from all directions as well as from the air. With some time before the assault was due to start they settled down and made some tea while Bert sat back enjoying a cigarette. He longed for some decent food but bully beef and biscuits were better than nothing, even if the biscuits were always stale and rock hard.

It was still warm, the September sun shone brightly in the almost cloudless blue sky. The earlier rain clouds had long since gone and to Bert it felt like a warm summer's day. It was surprisingly quiet, the only sounds were from the skylarks singing somewhere high in the sky above them and the odd scurrying sound in the undergrowth denoting the movement of a rabbit or vole. The silence was hypnotic and if it wasn't for the knowledge that at any minute the BEF barrage would begin Bert could have relaxed enough to have fallen asleep in the hazy warmth. But knowing the action would soon start he was alert; his senses aware of every sound.

At the expected time the BEF artillery opened up, shattering the silence with the rhythmic booming of the heavy guns as they powered their enormous shells over the heads of the Allies and onto the German positions. The noise was like nothing on earth. The ground shook and clods of earth could be seen flying skywards as the numerous shells buried themselves deep in the enemy front line killing and maiming those who were anywhere near. The whistling of the shells as they went over was nerve racking enough, but the noise as they hit the ground was even worse. Bert resisted the temptation to put his hands over his ears and instead began making sure his gun was ready to fire.

As the BEF artillery finished shelling there was a sudden deafening silence and then a faint cheering in the distance as the infantry assault began. Based at ninety degrees to the assault troops Bert had a perfect view as the infantry surged over the top of their trenches and ran full pelt, bayonets fixed, towards the German lines. Having decided in advance where his first rounds would go Bert began to fire, the short sharp bursts arcing towards the enemy in front of the advancing infantry. As his friends began cooling the gun and making sure he had a constant supply of ammunition he looked straight ahead, maintaining his aim and making sure the fire was not threatening the front line of the infantry, who by now had almost reached the German lines.

The sudden loud explosion to his right deafened him and almost sent him flying into the bottom of the trench, but somehow he steadied himself.

There was no time to look round before the next shell landed harmlessly behind him showering him in dirt, stones, mud and foliage. To his horror the artillery now appeared to have the correct range as the next shells landed perilously close, so close one of his friends completely disappeared and…at this point Bert had switched off his thoughts and opened his eyes. There was no point dwelling on his friends, two of whom had not survived the intense bombardment and one who had died painfully from his wounds before help could be summoned.

Deciding it was pointless to try and sleep he had then concentrated his attention on the countryside passing by his train window. There was little sign of the war here, the roads were quiet with no troops, guns or wagons moving equipment. There were no craters or fields of dead bodies. Instead the fields were freshly ploughed ready for the new planting, there were orchards with farmers picking the fruit from the heavily laden fruit trees. They were a poignant reminder of home and the farms around Walton on the Naze and he wondered what was happening back home, whether they knew what was happening just across the Channel.

When war had been declared back in August 1914 there had been celebrations in the streets the length and breadth of Britain and Walton on the Naze had been no exception. But not everyone had celebrated. Emma, like many who had lost their men to previous wars, could see nothing to celebrate. The war would mean her beloved Bertie would be sent abroad to a foreign country to fight. Emma could remember another war which everyone had celebrated and said would be over by Christmas. That war had lasted nearly three years and had taken her husband. Although she said nothing as it was considered to be unpatriotic not to support the war, she was terrified that this war would take away her only son.

She had seen him briefly before he left for France and he had reminded her so much of his father before he left for South Africa that it was like taking a step back in time. It was all she could do not to quarrel with him, but she did not want him knowing the depth of her sadness so she smiled and laughed and tried to join in with his enthusiasm which seemed to have no bounds. Inside her heart was breaking and as she watched him board the train to go back to London, she could barely stop the tears from flowing.

She left the station and headed home. But for once she couldn't face the empty cottage, so instead she went onto the crowded promenade and stood silently watching the waves crashing against the shore. The beach was full

Herbert Columbine VC.

Herbert Columbine VC.

Emma Columbine, Herbert's mother. *(Courtesy of Jean Pemberton, Emma's great-niece)*

St John's School, one of the schools Herbert attended as a child.

Melvin School, another school Herbert attended as a child.

The view of Silkaatsnek and the Crocodile River Crossing from the Western End of Rietfontein Camp. *(Courtesy of the South African Military History Association)*

Magaliesberg rock formations near Silkaatsnek.

Crescent Road in Walton where Emma and Herbert lived.

Walton Pier where Herbert may have worked.

Walton as it would have been when Emma and Herbert lived there.

CORPORAL

19th Hussars Hat Badge (after 1909) of the type Herbert would have worn.

19th Hussars uniform.

Complete set of brass service dress buttons Machine Gun Corps (Cavalry) belonging to Trooper Jago of the 19th Hussars, later Machine Gun Corps. *(Courtesy of the Combined Services Museum Maldon www.cmsm.co.uk)*

A Field Gun in France circa 1914.

A photo of some of the generals in France taken by a private soldier circa 1914.

An observation balloon over the trenches in France.

Preparing an observation balloon, France.

Clearing up after an enemy barrage.

A close up photo of a machine gun.

A member of the Machine Gun Corps training.

Vickers machine gun. *(Courtesy of The Rifles Living History Society www.riflebrigade.org.uk/)*

Another photo of the Machine Gun Corps training.

Machine Gun Corps arm patch.

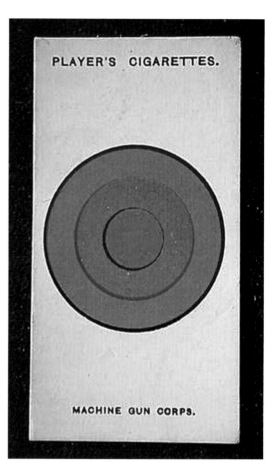

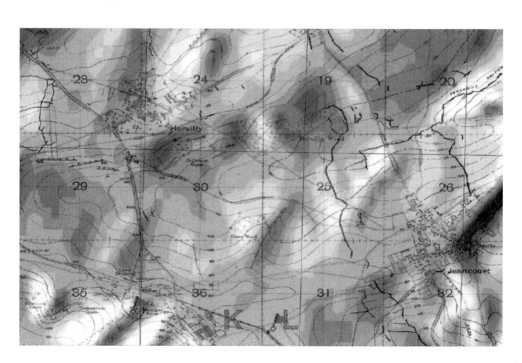

Pozieres Memorial.

The unveiling of the original memorial in Walton.

A photo of Emma at the unveiling of the original memorial.

Lord Byng of Vimy addressing the gathering at the unveiling of the original memorial.

The original memorial.

The original bust.

The original memorial in situ before it was vandalised.

Paying respects on Remembrance Day in the 1960s.

Honouring a local hero in the 1960s.

Saluting a local hero.

Drusilla Dundan – Emma's sister and Herbert's aunt. *(Courtesy of Jean Pemberton)*

A mock-up of the proposed memorial.

of people; there was a concert party on Albion Beach with Will Pepper's White Coons entertaining the large crowd and a sandcastle competition further down the beach. The bathing machines were all in use, the horse used to pull them up the beach standing bored with his owner as he waited patiently for the end of the day. But Emma was unaware of the happy, laughing people all around her. All she could see was Bertie in his smart dress uniform, waving to her out of the train window, the white smoke from the engine billowing around him and then he had gone, and she wondered if she would ever see him again.

Lost in his thoughts, it was only as the train pulled into Abbeyville station that Bert realized where he was. The train journey had catapulted back him into the past and reminded him of his last journey to Walton just before he had left England. He could still smell the sea air and see his mother's face as she waved goodbye to him on the platform and for the first time since he'd joined the army he realized why she had looked so sad.

Shrugging off his pessimistic thoughts and deciding it must be because he was tired, he grabbed his kit and detrained with the rest of the men onto the overcrowded French platform. Here they were ordered onto even more crowded buses and sent forward to the front line on the left of the French XXI Corps between Bethune-Fruges and Ypres. The rest of 'A' Squadron had gone ahead several days earlier to protect the arrival of the main infantry divisions. Together with the Cyclist Company reconnaissance patrols, outposts and advance guards were established to provide protection from enemy cavalry. Bert had travelled with his gun and the remaining men in his section.

Once they had begun digging in they were soon joined by reinforcements from St Omer and Anvers and the BEF began to establish a front which stretched from the north of Ypres to La Bassee. The intention was to try and turn the right flank of the German line, which now extended all the way back to Aisne. They were helped by the cavalry who extended the line past Merville and Hazebrouck to the high ground of the Monts des Flandres and to the canal near Ypres.

The land was flat with numerous drainage ditches and would prove difficult to defend and as the divisions moved forward the divisional cavalry screened their advance, engaging the enemy wherever it became necessary.

By the 12 October the French lost Vermelles, a small town on the edge of the Pas de Calais coal basin. This left Smith-Dorrien with a problem.

Should he move his forces north of the canal to attempt a north-easterly advance or move south to close the gap left by the French withdrawal and then advance in an eastwards direction? Having chosen the latter he placed II Corps south of the canal, apart from the five infantry brigades of the 3rd and 5th Divisions which he left facing four enemy cavalry divisions.

While Bert and the rest of the 5th Division held their line, the rest of II Corps began a slow advance and by the end of the day had reached the Noyelles-Givenchy-Lacouture line. The advance continued on the 13 October. However, there was no real result, although the heavy fighting and intense artillery bombardment left the British with around 1,000 casualties. The fighting on both sides of the canal continued on the 14 and 15 October with yet another 1,000 casualties, although heavy losses were also inflicted on the enemy. The British had advanced some six miles in four days and although the advance continued it now slowed considerably, thanks to a stiffening of German resistance. Givenchy was taken and held on the 16 October, and on the 17 October a foothold was gained on the Aubers Ridge. The advance continued eastwards and a bridge three quarters of a mile east of Givenchy was taken. This would be as far as they would get until 1918. The advance was halted by enemy fire from Brickstacks and the Railway Triangle and this eventually bought the advance on both sides of the canal to a standstill.

On the 19 October 300 men from the 2nd Royal Irish found themselves surrounded on the Aubers Ridge after a French defeat and had no option but to surrender. Two days later a German counter attack began, but after heavy fighting was repulsed by the 3rd Division. Eventually the Division gave up the Ridge as it was considered to be tactically untenable and by the 22 October the left of II Corps line found themselves exposed so they withdrew back to form a defensive front.

Further north the British retook Mont des Cats, Meteren and Mont Noir followed by Bailleul, Kemmel Hill and Messines. By the 14 October the 3rd Cavalry Brigade had met up with the Cavalry Corps south of Ypres and they had achieved their objective of establishing a continuous front from Ypres to La Bassee Canal. Three days later they had taken Armentieres.

By the 18 October 1914 the Western Front was complete. No further flanking movements were possible so the only way forward was straight through the enemy positions. On the same day the final gap in the allied front was closed as 7th Division reached Ypres and British troops entered the town. Ypres was a major centre in this part of Flanders and all the major roads converged on the town. Control of Ypres meant control of the surrounding countryside which was flat and criss-crossed with canals and rivers that linked it to the coast. The land to the south of the town known as the Mesen Ridge rose to about 500 feet high and would provide a significant advantage to the side that controlled it. Once in the town the BEF moved to the east and arrived at the Menin Road where they prepared to take part in the next offensive. They were unaware that a sizable German force was advancing towards them.

The First Battle of Ypres officially began on the 19 October when the Germans launched a general offensive that began on the Yser and spread south along the line. The 1st and 2nd Divisions of the BEF held firm all along the line from La Bassee to Langemarck and by the 22 October had managed to take the last section of the salient west of Langemarck. The French IX Corps was then bought in to replace the British 1st and 2nd Divisions and they occupied the whole of the northern half of the Ypres salient while the BEF held the line down to La Bassee. When the Germans threatened to break through at the end of October the French XV1 arrived to plug the gap. The battle continued with the French and the BEF changing roles, but between them they managed to hold the line, despite numerous German counter offensives.

The battle raged continually until November. There is no official end date but neither side were really able to dominate the other. The British and French continued to hold the line at Ypres and although fighting continued after the end of November it was not on such a large scale. The First Battle of Ypres ended with German casualties estimated at 134,315 with 19,530 dead, 83,520 wounded and 31,265 missing. Many of the German casualties at Ypres were from a volunteer corps who had been raised at the beginning of the war, including university students who had been exempt from the draft because they were at University. Twenty-five thousand of these students were killed at Ypres.

The British took 58,155 casualties between the 14 October and the 30 November. Of these 7,960 were dead, 29,562 wounded and 17,873 missing. The BEF had arrived in France with an infantry force of 84,000 men. By the end of the Battle of Ypres the BEF had taken 86,237 casualties.

As part of 'A' Squadron, Bert had found himself forming the advance guard for 3rd Division from the 10 October. Here they covered the left flank as they moved forward to the canal at Hinges. They continued to move forward with 3rd Division towards Herlies when they came across an enemy position. It was now the 18 October and having left the infantry to deal with the opposition they retired to their billets. On the 19 October they were sent in support of the Royal Irish and the 15th Hussars as they attacked Pilly. While the battle raged the troopers manned observation posts and reserve trenches until they rejoined 5th Division at Beuvry on 25 October. Two days later they were sent to search for snipers among the lines. Other than when they were supporting the infantry, such as on the 8 November when they were with 15th Brigade on the Ypres–Menin road, they moved around the Ypres district by horseback. When they were dismounted they sheltered their horses in the woods. Although there were great artillery duels taking place all around and aeroplane fights in the sky, from the 22 to 31 October 'A' Squadron were largely inactive as mounted cavalry.

As the Battle of Ypres drew to a close both 'A' and 'B' Squadrons found themselves digging support trenches and constructing fascines, while at night 'A' Squadron patrolled the telephone wires. Then, between November 1914 and April 1915, Bert found himself in the front line as 'A' Squadron took their turn to man the trenches.

Chapter 12

Winter of 1914

Bert huddled miserably into the far corner of the narrow trench trying to find some shelter. His uniform was soaked through by the torrential rain that never seemed to stop. He was cold and hungry and extremely fed up. The only good thing was that for the moment it was quiet, the Germans were huddled down into their trenches and probably just as miserable as him. The wind howled off the North Sea whipping the rain into horizontal lines that stung the parts of his face that were exposed and hammered noisily onto his army greatcoat which might have offered some warmth if it had been waterproof. The constant drip drip drip of the rain as it bounced off the gun barrel was almost as irritating as the rivers that flowed in torrents off the banks and into the bottom of the trench. He was knee deep in water and mud which was almost impossible to clear despite their best efforts and his feet were so cold he couldn't feel them at all. It was bad enough during the day, but at night, when they moved through the trenches in the dark, the water often hid bloated corpses that would rise up causing them to fall over.

He huddled down even more and tried to light a cigarette. It took three strikes of the match sheltered in his cupped hand to light it and he smiled wryly as he thought about the rhyme that was circulating. Never take the third light from a match as the German snipers used the match to perfect their aim.

Fortunately he was tucked well down in the trench so out of sight of the ruthless German snipers. It was his turn to rest while others kept watch. They were positioned several yards in front of the Allied line in a listening post in no-man's-land. The German front line was barely twenty yards away, so close that when the wind blew strongly enough he could hear them talking. He had no idea what they were saying, but he could hear their gruff guttural voices and occasional bursts of laughter, although what they could possibly find to laugh about was beyond him.

His machine gun section was so exposed that even getting into position had been very dangerous. After manoeuvring through the water logged trench system to its outer regions they had climbed warily over the top into no-man's-land. Here they had to crawl across yards of mud on their stomachs in the dark of the night, dragging their gun, ammunition and all the other equipment behind them. The heavy artillery had provided some covering fire while they dug in, but even though the bombardment was meant to keep the Huns' heads down there was always the danger of their lookouts spotting them. Their trench, located in front and to the side of the main trench system, was camouflaged with bushes and other greenery. In front of them they could see small crosses which warned where the ground was so bad that soldiers, overloaded with equipment, had sunk into the ground and drowned.

Sometimes he couldn't remember the young boy who had so longed to go to war. War was not how he'd imagined it at all and certainly not the exciting place his father had painted it to be. Bert often wondered whether his father had felt the same all those years ago, whether he too had lain awake at nights wondering how on earth he could have thought war was glamorous. But perhaps his father had enjoyed it. His letters had never said anything to the contrary so he could only assume that his father had not changed his mind.

The days were filled with murderous bombardments and suicidal infantry attacks in which neither side appeared to gain anything. Bert no longer felt anything as he fired his machine gun at the advancing hordes or in defence of his own infantry attacks. He was almost becoming used to the stench of the piles of rotting corpses that littered no-man's-land and immune to the cries of the wounded and dying of both sides. Almost, but not quite.

The nights were no safer. Although there were no massed attacks, snipers were very active as were patrols looking to capture prisoners. Exposed in a saphead Bert and his three companions were ever on the alert for movement from the German trenches that were so close to their position. The enemy also carried out other activities at night, directing bracketing fire on roads and communications and strafing the assembly points behind the front lines or 'suicide trenches' as they had become known.

He shivered again in the increasingly icy wind and wondered miserably if it was going to snow. It was certainly cold enough. He sipped the last dregs of his tea which was already cold even though it was hardly any time at all since he'd made it. But months in the BEF had taught him not to waste food. You never knew where the next supplies would come from or how long you would have to wait. Supplies of food and ammunition were at best intermittent and they were often reduced to eating their emergency rations. Several times they had run out completely.

But even worse than the hunger were the rats. Enormous, pink skinned and so fat from feeding off the corpses of the dead that they could no longer run, only waddle along the water-filled trenches. Their beady eyes would stare unblinkingly at the men as if they were eyeing them up for their next meal. They stole anything, he had even seen one sneaking off with a lighted candle in its mouth. To add to the horror their shrieks when cornered sounded like those of frightened children, a sound that could be heard echoing continuously round the trenches on both sides.

Bert closed his eyes and tried to sleep but it was too cold and his position, jammed up against the sodden muddy edge with water constantly dripping on him meant he kept dozing, only to jerk awake as one or other of his limbs went numb. Unable to sleep he found himself thinking back over the past few months and he realized that, however miserable he was, he was very lucky to still be alive. Machine gunners had suffered even higher casualty rates than those of the infantry and there were very few survivors by the winter of 1914.

Manning of the trenches and the listening posts was rotated. The men would normally spend one week in the front line trench followed by a week in a trench further back. The third week was spent in reserve at the back of the line so as Christmas 1914 approached Bert and his companions were taken out of the trenches, their positions now manned by some infantry machine gunners.

At first Bert couldn't work out whether he was pleased to be off the front line or whether he felt guilty that he was safe while others were fighting. But there were advantages to being a young man in France and it wasn't long before Bert was enjoying his excursions into nearby Ypres.

Back home Emma was facing another Christmas without Bert. Although she had become used to him being away from home over the past few years, his previous postings had been in England so he had been in little danger.

Now he was with the BEF she had no idea where he was and she had heard nothing from him since his first, hastily scribbled letter, sent not long after he had arrived in France. His obvious excitement reminded her poignantly of his father's first letter all those years ago. After reading it she had spent long hours standing on Marine Parade staring out to sea wondering where he was. It was very hot in the summer sun and normally she would have enjoyed breathing in the salty smell of kelp that wafted in from the sea. But for once the bracingly fresh air had failed to revive her spirits.

New businesses were still opening in Walton, and Stead and Simpson had just moved into the corner unit of Morton Terrace. But everywhere she went in Walton people were talking about the war and how it would soon be over. Many who knew her would ask for news of Bert and congratulate her for having such a brave son. Others, sensing her sadness, would comfort her by reminding her that it would all be over by Christmas. Despite the war the beaches were full of visitors enjoying the cooler air and the refreshing waves as they crashed noisily on the shore. Emma envied them their peace and sunny optimism as they queued for ice bricks and sticks of Walton rock at Hipkin's Refreshment Kiosk.

On the 8 August The Defence of the Realm Act, known as DORA, was passed. Although the first Act was quite short it introduced powers which controlled the British people in ways that had never happened before. Its original intention was to protect sensitive establishments and public buildings from sabotage but as the war progressed it was gradually amended and added to. It soon began to impose restrictions on people's movements, as well as their social and working lives. Civilians could now be arrested by the military and be subject to Courts Martial[1]. Together with rules about spreading rumours, communicating with the enemy and spreading disaffection the Act enabled the Government to requisition land and factories.

Further regulations introduced British Summer Time in September 1914 to give farmers more daylight hours and would be extended again in 1918 because of fuel shortages. Changes to Licensing Laws were also introduced as it was not considered to be fair that those at home should be out drinking while the men on the front line were fighting. In August 1914 the Military and Naval authorities were given the powers to close public houses and to restrict pub opening hours. Shortly after this the power was extended to civil authorities. By Christmas 1914 closing time in London was 10pm instead of 2.30am. Opening hours were further reduced in 1915 from sixteen to seventeen hours nationally (nineteen and a half hours in London) to five and a half hours and evening closing time became 9-9.30pm. By 1916 the Government, through the Central Control Board, (Liquor Traffic) had taken over several breweries and pubs because of concerns that drunkenness amongst the workers was endangering munitions factories.

Initially the papers reported that the BEF had joined with its ally France and successfully engaged the enemy. The papers were not allowed to report casualties or bad news so it wasn't until the 25 August when the newspapers first began to report that things were not going quite as well as they should have been. But still the public had little real idea of what was happening, even after headlines on the 30 August stating that British Regiments were broken and battling against the odds, and that more men were urgently needed. The government was determined that the public should not know the full extent of the retreat from Mons or the number of casualties so, as the newspapers were unable to report what was really happening, they resorted to fuelling anti-German feeling.

With little factual news Emma's imagination began to run riot, aided by the mass hysteria that was now gripping Britain, largely driven by the newspapers. Anti-German feeling had been bad enough before the beginning of the war, again, largely driven by the newspapers. As with the Boer War, increased literacy had provided large numbers of new readers for the newspapers who believed everything they read was the truth. Although cynicism would come later in the war, for now the majority believed that if it was in print it must be true. This suited the Government who, not having a large standing army, needed to recruit men in large numbers for the war. Despite this anti-German feeling however, *The Times* had still carried the front page advertisements put in by the German and Austrian Embassies in the week leading up to war. These requested the return home of all German and Austrian nationals who were old enough to fight.

On the 5 August the Alien Registration Act introduced emergency legislation which prevented enemy nationals from travelling without permits and requiring them to register at Police Stations. As the BEF left for France the national mood was cheerful. Buoyed up by the politicians and the media, the population seriously expected the war to be over by Christmas and for the victory to be relatively painless. But as things began to go against the BEF and they began to retreat after the defeat at Mons, the newspapers found it hard to find real news to put in the papers. Instead they began printing lurid tales of German atrocities. Nothing it seemed was too bad for the vicious Hun. From cutting off hands or breasts of young women to bayoneting babies to church doors, the papers were full of supposedly verified accounts by those who were there.

Although over 3,000 Germans were cited for war crimes after the war finished, many of the stories in the papers were unsubstantiated. But the general population were unaware of this and the German population of Britain, many of whom had been here many years were attacked and became the victims of outbreaks of vandalism and worse. Of the 53,000 plus Germans living in Britain at the beginning of the war only 22,000 remained at the end. Tens of thousands were interred in temporary buildings in Olympia and Alexandra Palace whilst others were sent to Holloway. Eventually some 30,000 of those in temporary accommodation were sent to the Isle of Man, to a camp at Knockaloe. Everything that had any connection with Germany was attacked or rejected. Dachshund dogs were attacked in the streets, German Shepherd dogs were renamed Alsatians, German measles was renamed Belgian Flush and German music was no longer played. German sausages and sauerkraut became anglicized and Boots the Chemist spent considerable amounts of time trying to persuade people that eau de Cologne was English and nothing to do with Germany.

When the war finished many thousands were deported, even those who had British wives and children and who considered themselves to be British in everything except name. There were widespread rumours of German spies, suspected plots to poison reservoirs and, for those living on the coasts, people supposedly signalling to ships at sea. The communities in the Great War were quite close knit so anyone who was not familiar or was a stranger was viewed with considerable suspicion and suspected of being a spy.

This became even worse after the 3 November 1914 when eight German Cruisers bombarded Yarmouth. With 600 miles of coastline on the east of the country it was virtually impossible for the Royal Navy, large as it was, to prevent every attack. Many of the militarily important towns, like Dover and Sheerness, had forts and guns. Hartlepool, a major ship building city, only had some minor gun emplacements which were hopelessly outclassed when up against the 11- and 12-inch guns of the German battleships and cruisers. But other east coast towns considered unimportant like

Scarborough, Yarmouth and Whitby were not considered to be targets, so remained largely unprotected.

This first attack against Yarmouth was unsuccessful mainly because the German Navy was worried about mines nearer the shore. They stopped ten miles from the coast and began firing, but the vast majority of their shells fell a long way short of the town. The bombardment was so inaccurate that large numbers of the population wandered down to the shore line to watch the flashes from the guns, followed by the columns of water rising into the air as the shells fell short and landed in the water. Because the town escaped any damage the authorities played it down. They also decided not to issue any instructions to the population in case of any other attacks as this might cause panic.

On the 16 December the German cruisers were back, this time Hartlepool, Scarborough and Whitby were their targets and this time they were considerably more successful. At 8.00am German shells hit the Grand Hotel in Scarborough as well as other private properties and churches. Whitby was also hit, followed by Hartlepool who bore the brunt of the attack. Over a period of fifty minutes approximately 1,500 shells were fired at the town. Although many failed to explode, some went into the sea and others overshot the town, the majority landed in and around the docks, hitting the gas and water works and the old town. Ninety-seven men and women, nine soldiers and thirty-seven children were killed, 446 were wounded and over 600 dwellings destroyed. With no instructions as to what they should do people had no idea whether to remain in their homes or whether to go into the streets. Some headed for the police station only to be led away from there as a direct hit would have caused enormous casualties. The authorities tried to play down the number of casualties and contain the news but by 4pm it had reached Essex.

Living in a coastal town the people of Walton would no doubt have been concerned about their own safety and would probably have looked to the armed forces to protect them. On the 14 November five or six submarines had been sighted at the mouth of the River Blackwater near Maldon, fuelling fears of invasion. There were field works all along the coast plus two batteries of light gun emplacements, four 15-pounders at Frinton and a further four at Clacton. Initially the authorities did not want to alarm the holiday makers but in February 1915 the London Defence Position was built. This largely followed the plans drawn up in the 1890s to bar the road from the coast to London from any invasion force that landed in East Anglia. Three trench systems were built, the outer running north of Chelmsford by Maldon and Danbury Hill while the inner trench ran via Ongar and Epping. If the Germans did land these trenches would be defended by fifty-three battalions of second line troops.

The 21st Battalion of Sherwood Foresters, a Home Defence force, were now billeted at Walton, some in private houses, others in Saville House which had a flat roof that flooded in wet weather. Soldiers could often be seen on the roof baling out the building with buckets. Others could be seen regularly drilling on the Naze. Their presence was both comforting to the local population and worrying as fear of invasion grew.

By now voluntary recruitment, which had reached its peak in August 1914, had tailed off. In the late summer and early autumn Kitchener made a direct appeal for more men, this time using his own image in the recruiting posters. The first hundred thousand men were recruited within a couple of days, but there was now a shortage of uniforms so in place of khaki they were given emergency blue serge uniforms. This was followed by the formation of the 'Pals Battalions', an idea introduced by Lord Derby who considered that men of the commercial classes might prefer to join up and fight with their 'pals', rather than with men of a different class and background with whom they had nothing in common.

The idea spread across the country rapidly, particularly in the industrial north and midlands where it became a matter of civic pride to raise, feed and equip a battalion until they were taken over by the War Office. Because there were no training camps yet most recruits remained living at home, either wearing civilian clothes or Kitchener's blue uniforms. The idea of the 'Pals Battalions' was so successful that by the end of 1914 there were 1,186,357 new recruits, all enthusiastically waiting to join the BEF.

Chapter 13

Christmas on the Front Line

As Christmas drew near the newspapers and magazines began a campaign to ensure troops on the front line were not forgotten. So successful was this that in the days leading up to the 12 December 1914, 250,000 parcels were sent to the troops. The following week there were another 200,000 parcels plus two and a half million letters. A further 2,500 letters were sent to British POWs. The King and Queen also sent every soldier, sailor and nurse a Christmas card and Princess Mary sent them all a Christmas present of a brass box filled with tobacco and other goods. Towns and villages also sent Christmas puddings, cigarettes and matches. These plus the extra letters and parcels took up considerable space on the trains. This meant food and other essentials were delayed, much to the exasperation of the generals.

Having sent her parcel and letter to Bert, Emma settled in for a quiet Christmas. She had taken to walking along the promenade every day and staring out to sea wondering how Bert was. As she took her daily walk on the 22 December the rhythmic crashing of the waves on shore that she normally found so soothing was interrupted by the sound of firing in the distance. Even to Emma's untrained ear it sounded like a real battle rather than the firing practice she had become used to hearing. But, despite staring for ages into the hazy distance, she could see nothing. The firing continued for a while and then faded away leaving her alone with her thoughts. The weather had now turned cold and wet and she was pleased to get back inside to her roaring fire. She could only hope that it would not be such a cold winter as some of the previous ones. In 1906, just after they had moved there, Walton had seen its heaviest snowfall in fifteen years. In 1908 and 1909 it had been so cold that the sea had frozen and the snow had continued to fall right up until March. The weather had been so bad that the Harwich and Frinton life boats had collided in the blizzard conditions. So far the snow had kept off and she could only hope it would stay that way. But as Christmas passed the weather deteriorated even more and on Monday 28 December there was a massive storm that bought down trees and telegraph wires in Thorpe Le Soken blocking the road.

Back in France life for the troops in the trenches remained cold, wet and generally unpleasant. The trenches were deep enough so the men could walk about without their heads showing. If they wanted to fire there were fire steps every few feet. These were just places where the trench had not been dug quite so deep. When the men wanted to fire they climbed up a couple of feet on the fire step and they could then see to shoot over. Although they were deep they did not provide complete protection as shells could still land in the trench and enfilade fire from the German pom-pom[1] gun along the top of the trench often caught those on sentry duty by surprise. Another danger came from snipers who were deadly accurate. Most regiments soon formed their own sniper sections, often those who had been big game hunters in civilian life.

Given the proximity between the two front lines there were many amicable exchanges between the sides. Men of both sides would gather in their separate trenches and sing the popular songs of the day while the other side would listen and often ask for encores. News was regularly exchanged and the 'Breakfast hour truce' became an almost accepted ritual in some parts of the Western front. A soldier would stick a board up in the air and all the firing would stop while both sides drew their water and rations, ate their food and paid their trips to the latrines.

But the men saved most of their singing for when they were marching away from the front line, the relief that they had survived another week palpable in every note. Many of the most popular songs were well known tunes with different words. *'We're here because, we're here, because, we're here because, we're here…'* was sang regularly with gusto to the tune of *Auld Lang Syne* and summed up the plight of most of the soldiers who had no real idea where they were or why they were there. Another popular song for those near Ypres was *Far, Far from Ypres* sung to a pre-war ballad called *Sing me to sleep*. *'Far, far from Ypres[2] I long to be, Where German snipers can't snipe at me, Damp is my dug out, Cold are my feet, Waiting for whizz bangs, To send me to sleep.'*

As the standard of British rifle marksmanship had declined with the loss of its experienced regulars the deficiency in machine guns became more obvious, at least to those in France. Britain's infantry firepower had been reduced by sixty per cent since the beginning of the war. The Germans on the other hand were using machine guns more and more, and BEF casualties had increased proportionately. The more foresighted of the generals realized that the pre-war regular army had been virtually obliterated. If they were to have any chance of winning they needed to invest in machine guns. They also needed to invest in specialist training. Thus the idea of a Machine Gun Corps was born.

On the 24 December 1914 the first school opened in the Caserne D'Abrot in St Omer. The first students to be selected as potential instructors were sixteen men from the Artists Rifles. From its inauspicious beginning the Machine Gun Corps grew from 470 officers and 170 other ranks in April 1915 to 159,000 officers and men by 1917. But in the winter of 1914 this was just the beginning and it would not be until 27 June 1916 that Bert and sixty-nine men from the 19th Hussars would be compulsory transferred to the MGC Cavalry.

Although there were no major attacks leading up to Christmas things were by no means quiet. From Sir John French's HQ the following message was sent out 'It is thought possible that the enemy may be contemplating an attack during Xmas or New Year. Special vigilance will be maintained during these periods.'[3] It's not clear whether this message was sent out because there were fears of a surprise attack or because there were concerns that there might be some signs of friendliness between the front line troops and HQ wanted to make it clear that this would be disapproved of.

In Germany families were also encouraged to send troops Christmas trees and other reminders of home. Most Germans in the trenches were looking forward to a more peaceful time when they could think about their families back home. Bringing Christmas trees into the house had originated in Germany and the tradition had spread to Britain when Albert married Queen Victoria, although by 1914 it was still not widespread. In preparation for Christmas the Germans had begun decorating their trenches and dugouts with Christmas trees and had even decorated parts of their parapets with small trees hung with candles. On Christmas Eve in some places along the line the Germans began shouting across no-man's-land. Some British Regiments responded by just throwing tins of food across the open space whereas in other places men climbed out of their trenches, met in the middle, shaking hands, sharing photos of their families and exchanging small items such as tobacco and food. Burial parties were sent out and time was spent repairing dugouts and trenches.

In some places football matches are believed to have taken place, although accounts vary as to where and how many. But what is not in doubt is that in several places along the front line, men who had been trying to kill each other only days earlier, were now shaking hands and making friends. As the arrangements for the truce were made locally, the length of time it lasted varied. In some places it was only a few hours, but in others it lasted until New Year's Day. However, there were exceptions. Pte Ernest Palfrey of 2nd Bn Monmouthshire Regiment was killed on Christmas Day while returning from a burial party. This was despite being in an area where a truce had been agreed and where fraternization was happening.

As in the 2nd Boer War the troops wrote letters home and many were sent on to the newspapers. After Christmas 1914 the newspapers began printing letters from the troops describing the 'Christmas truce'. This horrified the War Office as it was quite obvious that an unofficial truce had taken place and there had been considerable fraternization between the troops. Despite it being obvious that the truce was a result of humanity rather than treachery, there were considerable repercussions which reverberated all the way up the military chain of command. The death penalty was then introduced as a penalty for fraternization and to make sure it never happened again.

As January 1915 approached the snow arrived and the men found themselves enduring icy conditions as the winter took hold. Weapons froze and icicles hung from the machine guns. The ground was at least hard now that it was frozen and the men could walk about more easily. They could even sleep, but when they slept their boots would freeze to their feet. This was excruciatingly painful. They also found that their greatcoats froze in the icy conditions as did any yellow clay that was on them. This made them very heavy and as stiff as a board. In many cases the men hacked off the bottom two feet of their coats with their bayonets and walked about in short coats instead.

Trench foot became a common condition and the hospitals were full of sufferers. Initially thought to be a problem of poor morale it was soon accepted that the conditions in the trenches were ideal for trench foot to spread. Some 20,000 British soldiers were reputed to have trench foot by the end of 1914. Caused by the feet being submerged in cold water for hours at a time they became numb, swollen and turned red. Blisters and sores appeared, which became infected with fungi, and the feet then turned blue. Unless there was prompt treatment the whole foot could become gangrenous, resulting in amputation.

Doctors would stick needles into the feet of those affected and they would be completely unaware and unable to feel it. When the feeling eventually returned it was so agonizingly painful that the men were often unable to walk on them at all. They were given no help so would have to crawl around on their hands and knees when needing to get to the toilet. In an attempt to reduce the number of cases, soldiers were ordered to carry three pairs of dry socks with them and change their socks three times a day. Drainage in the trenches was also improved and the number of cases gradually reduced.

The Battle of Neuve Chappelle fought between the 10 and 13 March 1915 marked the beginning of a new year of fighting for the British and was supposed to have been part of a wider offensive in the Artois region. But troops who were meant to relieve those at Ypres had been redirected to Gallipoli instead, so the action was undertaken unilaterally. The decision to attack was made by Sir John French, Commander in Chief of the BEF. While the British were attacking there the French were supposed to attack the village of Aubers, a mile to the east. The aim was to press the German defence of Lille and reduce the small German salient near Neuve Chapelle.

The attack began at 6.55am on the 10 March with a thirty-five minute artillery bombardment of 342 guns using more shells than in the whole of the Boer War. The artillery was directed by eighty-five Reconnaissance Aircraft from the Royal Flying Corps. At 7.30am, once the bombardment stopped, 40,000 men from Haig's First Army advanced along a three kilometre front.

The objective of the battle had been to break through the German trench system at Neuve Chappelle and take the village of Aubers. The cavalry were to wait behind the line so that if a gap appeared they could ride through it and exploit the open countryside. The infantry reached the German support line with little difficulty and then, after four hours of hand to hand fighting, they captured the village. But the communication system was bad and the telephone line had been shelled. This meant a gap of five hours while the infantry waited for orders to advance further. By the time orders came through the element of surprise had gone and the Germans had moved fresh troops into the area. On the 12 March the Germans launched a massive counter attack. The British managed to hold on, but were unable to advance any further towards Aubers. The artillery bombardment hadn't reached Aubers and the front line wire here was intact. Of the 1,000 troops who attacked Aubers none survived. The advance was called off on the 13 March.

For the soldiers it was a foretaste of what was to come and it also gave them a new song; *'We beat 'em on the Marne, we beat 'em on the Aisne, they gave us hell at Neuve Chapelle but here we are again'* was now sung loudly to the tune of *Coming through the rye* as the lucky survivors marched away from the front line.

Back at HQ French blamed the shortage of artillery shells and decided that a thirty-five minute bombardment was not long enough. In future engagements artillery bombardments should be much longer. Unfortunately this decision would only add to the loss of lives as the extension of the bombardment took away the vital element of surprise and allowed the Germans to bring up reserves to the area under fire.

On the 11 March the British newspapers carried the story of the successful battle of Neuve Chappelle which had taken place the day before. On the 13 March Field Marshal John French's dispatch was also published. This too told of British success, the effectiveness of the heavy artillery, the mutual support afforded by the battalions involved and that casualties were not great in proportion to the ground that had been gained.

However, like most people, Emma was sure the news the papers carried was misleading. The main reason for these doubts were that most people considered the best way to judge a battle's success was by the number of casualties. As casualty lists were getting longer each day rumours that the press were lying were growing.

There was some justification for their cynicism as after three days of fighting the British had taken a piece of German land that totalled 2,000 yards by 1,200 yards. The price of this victory was over 7,000 British casualties and over 4,000 Indian casualties. The Germans lost a similar number and 1,200 German troops were captured by the British. Haig had achieved a clean break in the German lines, something that would only happen twice more in the whole of the war. Yet poor communications meant he had not fully exploited it. Instead he ordered more frontal attacks in the next two days which led to heavy casualties while precious little ground was gained.

The public continued to blame both the Government and the press for the lack of information. But the journalists were hampered by lack of co-operation from the military. While the Battle of Neuve Chappelle took place most correspondents sent their reports from somewhere in Northern France whilst trying to avoid arrest. Even those invited to join the British HQ in France saw very little of the battle as they were told there was no room on the front line for anyone who wasn't holding a gun. Instead they were given reports on how the British HQ in France functioned on a daily basis. Not realizing that they knew nothing about the first British offensive of 1915 which was taking place outside British HQ, the journalists were lulled into such a false sense of security that they even wrote in their reports that very little was hidden from them.

A month later there was public outcry when the public found out the truth. French blamed the government for lack of shells, the government blamed the munitions workers and some papers blamed Kitchener. French hastily brought out another dispatch which was completely different from his first one. This time he blamed Haig and other generals for not bringing up the reserves quickly enough.

The public had now lost faith in the government and the military. Even more discouraging they had lost trust in the press to bring them accurate reports. Emma no longer had faith in the news she was reading and she feared for the safety of her son, but then things took a turn for the worse.

In April 1915 the whole of the 19th Hussars were concentrated again as one unit in the 9th Cavalry Brigade which was part of the 1st Cavalry Division and in May they found themselves in the thick of the fighting at the Battle of Frezenberg Ridge and at Bellewaarde Ridge. Here they encountered a terrifying new weapon.

Chapter 14

Frezenberg Ridge

The Second Ypres Offensive began on the 22 April with the first large scale gas attack on the Western Front and lasted until the 25 May. It was primarily a series of fierce battles that took place between small opposing units. One of these actions was the Battle of Frezenberg Ridge which took place between the 8 and 13 May 1915.

In early April 1915 units of Smith-Dorrien's 2nd Army had arrived to support the extension northwards of the British lines. But at the same time these British troops were returning to the Ypres Salient, the Germans had begun an assault to take the high ground around Pilckem and Langemarck.

Just before 5pm on the 22 April the Germans began bombarding the trenches between Yser canal and Langemarck with their 17-inch Howitzers. This was followed almost immediately by the release of 5,700 canisters containing 168 tons of chlorine gas in the direction of the trenches. These trenches were manned by two French Divisions of French Algerian and territorial troops. Within minutes a greenish yellow mist began rolling towards the French positions from the German lines.

Completely defenceless against the gas the French troops fled towards Ypres in panic leaving the trenches clogged with the heavy gas which had sunk where it had gathered. It eventually covered four miles of the trenches and half of the 10,000 troops affected died of asphyxiation within ten minutes of the gas reaching the front line. The survivors found themselves temporarily blinded and about 2,000 were captured. This allowed the Germans to occupy Langemarck and Pilckem and threaten Steenstraat and Het Sas on the canal. It also left a four mile gap on the left of the nearest British forces who happened to be a Canadian Division.

As the gas began to dissipate the German infantry began to advance. Despite wearing primitive respirators they advanced carefully, expecting to find traps left behind by the retreating French. But their caution was unnecessary. The gas attack meant the French had fled without preparing any defensive devices. Fortunately for the Allies the success of the attack had also taken the German infantry by surprise and the actual breakthrough was not fully exploited.

Urgently needing to breach the gap, the Canadians secured a defensive line by improvising scattered outposts overnight. Despite numerous gas attacks and relentless shell fire they refused to give ground and the next day they launched several counter attacks. This prevented the Germans from advancing any further than just under two miles into the Allied Lines. As the counter attacks increased in ferocity the Germans came to a halt.

Unable to advance any further they began digging in to their newly won ground while Smith-Dorrien appealed to the French to counter attack. The French promised an attack the following morning, so, under the cover of darkness, the Canadians launched a surprise attack and successfully seized Kitchener's Wood[1], albeit with numerous casualties. But the French attack never materialized, so under heavy shell fire they had no option but to withdraw back to the southern edges of the wood.

Anticipating further German attacks, the British scraped together as many reserves as they could throughout the night. In the early morning of the 23 April they tried unsuccessfully to dislodge the Germans from Mauser Ridge. Although they did manage to establish a line of sorts within 1,200 yards of the canal it came at the cost of many casualties. The French now requested GHQ to order an attack on Pilckem. As they were still expecting the French to counter attack GHQ ordered 13th Brigade to advance towards Pilckem. With virtually no preparation and no reconnaissance and little idea of exactly where the enemy was it was a total disaster. The highly visible advancing troops were cut down by machine gun, rifle fire and heavy shelling and took over 2,000 casualties. Having gained virtually no ground, all forward movement was halted within three hours of the attack being launched.

On the 24 April the Germans begun a heavy bombardment of the British and Canadian lines and discharged more gas. Although the British and Canadians withstood repeated attacks with little protection against the gas, they were eventually driven back and by the afternoon the Germans had passed St Julian. In panic at losing so much ground the French made repeated requests to the British to counter attack. The next few days followed the same pattern as the previous ones, with numerous unsuccessful counter attacks by the British, supposedly with support from the French which was either late or ineffectual.

Having suffered so many costly defeats Smith-Dorrien approached Field Marshal French and called for permission to withdraw to a tenable defensive line. This resulted in French replacing him with General Plumer. However, Plumer also agreed with the need to pull back to a better defensive line, but the retreat was again delayed because the French General Foch pleaded with them not to concede any more ground. It was only after the disastrous counter attack by the French on the Yser canal line on the 1 May, followed by a further gas attack on the 2 May, that the British forces were finally able to withdraw back to a new line three miles from Ypres. The Canadians had suffered heavy losses with 5,975 casualties including 1,000 dead and the loss of the high ground to the north had significantly weakened the Allied position.

Delighted by the retreat of the British forces the Germans moved their artillery forward and prepared for an attack on Frezenberg Ridge. On the 8 May at 5.30am the Germans began a massive bombardment on the vulnerable British forward trenches on the slopes of the ridge. The subsequent infantry attack was repelled by the British as was the second attack, but the third attack, on either side of the village, caused the defenders to fall back. 80th Brigade[2] on the right flank managed to halt the German advance, but on the left flank 84th Brigade[3] was almost totally destroyed. By the afternoon the Germans had succeeded in creating a two-mile gap in the British lines. In response the British hastily improvised a series of counter attacks and managed to rescue the situation, but on the 9 May the Germans began a series of attacks further south. Despite the ferocity of the bombardments the defenders held on and the German advance was finally halted.

The 19th Hussars had spent the past couple of days since the 8 May in their billets before being brought forward ready to support the rest of the Cavalry Force if needed. At 7pm on the 10 May the 8th Cavalry Brigade, who had been waiting in reserve at Brielen, had sent dismounted parties forward to the Hooge Chateau. Their aim was to take over the trenches that were located near the Chateau. But as they neared the trenches their orders were changed and they returned back to their billets in Brielen, arriving at 7.30am on the morning of the 12 May.

The rest of the day was relatively quiet other than the heavy German artillery bombardment on 27th Division's positions. As night fell the 1st and 3rd Cavalry Divisions were mobilized and sent to replace 28th Division who had suffered severe casualties after three weeks of very heavy fighting.

The 19th Hussars had fought as part of the 1st Cavalry Division until the 12 May when, having taken up position in the trenches, they were re-designated Cavalry Force 2nd Army. Attached to them were artillery and engineering units of 28th Division and they were all placed under the command of Temporary Major-General Henry De B De Lisle CB, DSO. Each cavalry brigade consisted of between 800 and 900 men with fifty officers and was equivalent to a full strength infantry unit.

During the night of the 11/12 May the 8th Cavalry Brigade moved up in reserve to the 3rd Cavalry Division. They were now minus the Essex Yeomanry who had been sent to dig a communication trench south-east of Potijze. The Brigade was occupying support trenches in the line east of Potijze and providing a reserve to the 7th Cavalry Brigade who were located in trenches to the left of the line. The 6th Cavalry Brigade was occupying the trenches to the right of the line. Thus the cavalry now occupied the line from Bellewaarde Lake to Wieltje.

On the 13 May the 8th and 9th Brigade were still waiting in reserve. For Bert this at least meant some time away from the dangerous front line. But although they were in reserve this was not a time to relax. Instead he used the time to clean his machine gun which was continually clogged with the thick glutinous mud that surrounded them. One of the main problems was the tendency for the belts to get wet which caused more than seventy-five per cent of its failures in the trenches. Trying to keep them dry in the incessant rain was a constant challenge, but it could save his life and those of his comrades.

As the day wore on the rain fell relentlessly turning the shallow trenches into a quagmire of churning mud, but all was relatively quiet and Bert allowed himself to hope that it might remain so. The rain continued through the night and by the early hours of the morning they were knee deep in water. Then, at 4.00am the peace was shattered as the German artillery opened up and began shelling them. The bombardment was so intense that before long it had totally demolished the rather inadequate trenches of the 7th Cavalry Brigade. The bombardment continued unabated and began to spread outwards. It was now covering a full mile which meant it was now falling on the positions of the 6th Cavalry Division, the 2nd Dragoon Guards (Queens Bay's), 1st Cavalry Brigade 1st Cavalry Division.

Even from their positions in the rear the devastation in front of them was obvious. The air around them was filled with a pall of thick acrid smoke that caught in their throats and made their eyes water. This was bad enough but at least there was no gas. Through the thick gritty smoke Bert could just about make out houses collapsing and trenches subsiding as the bombardment seemed to intensify. The noise was deafening as the artillery shells pounded the landscape leaving giant craters in their wake. As the shells landed enormous mounds of mud, stones and other debris flew skywards before returning to earth causing even more devastation. Everywhere Bert looked there were dead and dying men, their limbs shattered by the devastating shelling. He closed his eyes briefly and offered up a quick prayer, then reluctantly opened them again. Despite their relatively safe position at the rear there was no knowing when they would be ordered to relieve a beleaguered trench or counter attack.

Although he would not have thought it possible, after two hours the barrage began to intensify even more. Eventually shells began to fall on the positions of the 8th Cavalry Brigade in the rear. Back at the front line the bombardment was now so heavy that despite a spirited defence the German infantry had begun to overrun the British trenches.

The 8th Cavalry Brigade began preparations for a counter attack. On their left flank would be the 10th Hussars, on their right the Royal Horse Guards and they would be supported by the Essex Yeomanry. The British 28th Divisional Artillery was now very low on ammunition and their guns were worn out, but at 2pm they began a barrage of their own.

As the barrage rained down on the enemy positions the Essex Yeomanry and Royal Horse Guards began advancing on the right of the line. It was 2.20pm. With their heads down and bayonets fixed they began running across the churned up, swirling mud towards the enemy. But it very quickly became apparent that they had gone before the allocated time for the attack, which was 2.30pm. The attack was halted briefly while they waited for permission to advance. But as they waited the shout suddenly went up that the enemy was withdrawing. Instantly the whole line began to move forward. Men rose from their dugouts and the Hussars began the long advance to the enemy positions across the churned up mud. Immediately they found themselves under intense rifle fire, but with minimal casualties they were able to reach and recapture the line. But almost immediately the

Germans began a counter attack and before long they were on the receiving end of a very accurate and intense German barrage. Despite their attempts to consolidate the line they found themselves increasingly under pressure. They had lost communication with the other units and every runner they sent failed to get through.

The rain was falling even heavier than before and the mud began clogging their rifles rendering them inoperative. On the high ground around Verlorenhoek the Germans could be seen massing and preparing for yet another assault, but somehow they still held on. By 4.30pm they were finally ordered to retire to a position about 600 yards to the rear of the reverse slope of Verlorenhoek ridge. But once the Hussars left the trench they became even more vulnerable. They had hardly covered any distance before they found themselves subject to a fierce enemy artillery bombardment which caused heavy casualties. The survivors, just five officers and ninety-eight other ranks, eventually managed to limp back to the relative safety of the dugouts they had occupied before the attack. Here they continued to provide support to the right flank of the 2nd Dragoon Guards until 10.30pm when they were relieved by the 9th Cavalry Brigade.

As Bert and the 9th Cavalry Brigade moved up the line they passed the remnants of the 8th and Bert found himself praying that they too would not be subject to such a fierce battle. But as they moved into the dugouts recently vacated by the 8th he had little time to think. With the rest of his troop he made his way through the waterlogged trench to the edge where they began to set up the machine gun. They had received so much practice that this took hardly any time and within minutes they were ready. Trying to ignore the rain and the mud Bert settled into position and tried to make himself as comfortable as he could; and then he waited.

But things had quietened, the battle for Frezenberg Ridge was over. After six days of intense fighting the Germans had gained a mere 1,000 yards of front between Hooge and Mouse Farm. Although it was seen as an unqualified success for the Germans, because they had gained a slice of the salient about a mile deep, casualties were so high that further offensive operations were halted.

The 9th Cavalry Brigade remained in position until they were relieved by the 2nd Dragoons (Scots Greys) of the 5th Cavalry Brigade, 2nd Cavalry Division at 8.30pm on the evening of the 14 May. Bert had survived another day.

Chapter 15

The First Battle of Bellewaarde

The beginning of 1915 had not been any better back home either. The winter had been the wettest on record with parts of Essex having 150 per cent of their normal rainfall. On the 19 January 1915 the Germans launched a Zeppelin raid on Great Yarmouth in Norfolk. Its target was the Humber, but having arrived close to Great Yarmouth it dropped its first bomb in a field. From there it flew over the town and then dropped several more bombs, killing two people. The raid only lasted ten minutes even though it took the Zeppelin over twenty-three hours to make the trip there and back from Germany. It was followed by a further twenty-six raids in January, and each time they attacked nervousness and fear grew. The government and press were in a quandary, not sure whether to draw attention to them so they could publicly condemn the attacks on women or children, or whether they should keep such reports low key, for fear of raising the level of public anxiety.

The first air raid over London took place on the 31 May 1915. Zeppelin LZ38, under the command of Captain Linnarz, dropped 3,000 pounds of explosive on the capital killing seven people and wounding thirty-five. On the 18 June the first air raid precautions were announced but it was up to local military authorities to decide whether they should impose a blackout. The blackout normally just meant dimming the lights before an attack. On the roads the tops of gas lights were painted with a pinkish coloured paint so that any light only pointed downwards. The blackout immediately led to a rise in the number of accidents as people bumped into each other and objects as they couldn't see where they were going.

The newspapers were starved of accurate war news by government restrictions introduced as part of The Defence of the Realm Act which prevented them from printing news that would cause despondency. Inevitably they filled the papers with whatever news they could find at home so the significance of the raids was blown completely out of proportion. The effect of this was to ensure that more troops were kept in Britain to prevent invasion instead of being sent to France. Furthermore, money was spent on providing adequate defence against the raids. Eight Warning Control Centres were built in the major cities to receive reports from the coastal stations and the police. Home Defence Stations were also set up with aircraft stationed in Britain ready to react to the reports received from the Warning Centres. Seventeen thousand three hundred men were placed on anti-aircraft duties as searchlight stations were set up from Edinburgh to Dover, all supported by anti-aircraft guns.

These searchlights were used more to blind the pilots of the Zeppelins, rather than provide a target for the anti-aircraft guns. The guns were invariably relics from the Boer War and most were unable to fire high enough to hit the airships. The shells would explode well below them and cover the neighbouring streets in shards of metal. But they also provided re-assurance to the public that something was being done to protect them.

Warnings of air raids were also inadequate, although as the crews of the Zeppelins themselves often had no idea where they were likely to end up, this was hardly surprising. Even in London, where lighting restrictions had been in place since September 1914, there was no real warning procedure in place. A policeman would come round on his bike, ringing his bicycle bell with a notice on saying 'take cover'. Constables also walked round shouting 'take cover' or blew whistles. When it was safe they would shout 'all clear' and people would return to their beds. There were virtually no municipal air raid shelters and people were advised to take cover in cellars or lie down if they were in the open. Those without cellars sheltered under the stairs as this was traditionally the strongest part of the building.

Although Zeppelin attacks continued in Suffolk (Ipswich, 30 April 1915 and Woodbridge, 14 August 1915), Essex (Southend, 10 May 1915, Burnham and Latchingdon, 29 May 1915), and London (8 September 1915), Walton le Soken was not hit. But although Emma was safe she still worried about her sisters who were living in London.

On the 23 April the shock headlines 'Poison gas used by enemy helps them to advance' appeared. Although subsequent accounts in the papers varied as to how long lasting the effects were most people found the use of gas morally repugnant. For those like Emma, who had relatives on the front line, it was just something else to worry about.

Back in Europe Bert and the rest of the 1st Cavalry Division (1st and 2nd Cavalry Brigades) were now part of 83rd Brigade which in turn formed part of the V Corps Front. By 24 May this front extended from about five-and-a-half miles from Hill 60 in the south to the flank of French forces close to Turco Farm in the north. The 1st Cavalry Division was located on either side of the Menin road east of Hooge which was on the south of the line. The 4th Yorks Battalion section and the 9th Lancers were also defending the position astride the Menin Road at Hooge. With the Cavalry Corps were the York and Durham Brigade who were defending the line west of Bellewarde Lake. The centre of the front, across the railway line and reaching to the Ypres-Zonnebeke Road, was occupied by the 85th Brigade. The area from Wieltje to Mouse Trap Farm[1] was occupied by 10th Brigade and the northern flank, as it curved west towards Turco Farm, was occupied by 12th Brigade.

The continuous heavy rain since the 14 May had made living conditions difficult for the troops in the front line. The rain had hindered trench repairs, but there had been some improvement in protection against gas attacks. Gas helmets made of flannel bags with eye pieces were issued to machine gunners first and vermoral[2] sprays were introduced to neutralize any remaining traces of the chlorine gas that was lingering in the trenches.

The weapons available to the men in the trenches were still woefully inadequate. The trench mortars at their disposal were either very old or hastily improvised. Some were made of iron, others of brass and many were more dangerous to those firing them than the enemy. The hand grenades were also basic and the most popular of the improvised models had been nicknamed the 'jam pot', 'Battye bomb' and 'hairbrush' by the men.

As its name implies the 'jam pot' bomb was made from an empty jam pot. This was filled with shredded gun cotton and ten penny nails, a No 8 detonator and short length of Bickford's fuse wire. The lid would be clamped up and lit with a match, lighter or cigarette before being thrown at the enemy.

The 'Battye bomb' was a cast iron cylinder about four inches by two, filled with ammonal. It was closed with a wooden plug with a hole through its centre in which the detonator and fuse were inserted.

The 'hairbrush' was made by sticking some gun cotton to a slab of wood, shaped like a hairbrush, and ignited in the same way the jam pot was. The enemy were much better prepared and had proper trench mortars, hand and rifle grenades and rifles with telescopic sights which were ideal for snipers. There was also constant danger from the German howitzers whose shells came over in a looping trajectory.

The last battle of the 2nd Ypres Offensive, the Battle of Bellewaarde, took place on the 24 and 25 May 1915. At 2.45am on the morning of 24 May the Germans launched a massive artillery bombardment along the length of the line. The air was filled with the noise of shells, rifle fire and machine guns and then the Germans released some more gas. Great grey-yellow clouds of the noxious chlorine gas rose forty feet high in the sky and began to waft slowly towards the British lines. Although they had been expecting a gas attack, because of the favourable wind everything happened so quickly that many men did not have time to put on their masks and were completely overcome. The gas drifted onwards and even those some twenty miles behind the front experienced it. The bombardment was followed almost immediately by a German infantry assault. Despite the gas the attack was beaten off, in many cases by the rifle and machine gun fire of the determined British defenders. The attack continued until 7am but the line held firm.

But Mouse Trap Farm in the north, located half a mile from Wieltje, was reduced to a heap of rubble after the bombardment on the 24 May. Positioned only thirty yards from the enemy trenches, it was almost inevitable that the two platoons of Dublin Royal Fusiliers, tasked with defending it, were almost immediately overrun. In the south German infantry also managed to break into the British line both north and south of Bellewaarde Lake.

Unable to muster sufficient troops for a counter attack the British could not retain Mouse Trap Farm. The ground was so waterlogged that any trenches that were dug immediately filled with water and mud and, although the French offered some of their troops, they were later declared to be unavailable. It was finally decided at nightfall to withdraw back to a more defensible line above Wieltje.

At Bellewaarde Lake the Germans had managed to break into the Allied line. Desperately needing more men the 84th Brigade were called in, but they did not arrive until early evening, having endured a gruelling cross country march on empty stomachs. On the way there they came under repeated attack by German artillery and many men were killed or wounded before even reaching Bellewaarde. On arrival they immediately attacked Witte Poort Farm and successfully evicted the Germans from both the farm and the ridge below. They then dug in to await the arrival of 80th Brigade. When 80th Brigade finally arrived the two brigades made a joint counter attack at 11pm; unfortunately it was a bright moonlit night and the men were easy targets for the well dug in Germans. It was a complete disaster with both brigades suffering heavy casualties. The battle had finished by early morning and the following day there was a reduction in shelling. From this point the Germans made no attempt to launch any more offensives.

The German advance had forced an Allied withdrawal, even though very little extra ground was ceded. But the German attack had considerably reduced the size of the Allied salient. The highest ground had been lost and it was now no more than three miles across and five miles deep.

The Battle of Bellewaarde marked the end of the 2nd Ypres Offensive leaving nearly 60,000 British dead, missing and wounded. The British casualties were the highest with 59,275 officers and men killed, missing or wounded. Of these 10,519 officers and men were killed. French losses were around 10,000 while German losses amounted to about 35,000 killed, missing or wounded. The main reason Allied losses were so high was the use by the Germans of chlorine gas.

But the Germans had now run low on supplies so they turned their attention to the town of Ypres which they began bombarding mercilessly. With the British Army camped in and around the town it was an obvious target.

About 8,000 German troops had initially passed through Ypres on the 7 October 1914. They raided the town's coffers, ordered thousands of loaves of bread to be baked, and left the following day. Within three weeks of the German's brief visit they carried out a major offensive to try and go back to the town. Despite being outnumbered the British held their line, counter attacked at Gheluveld at the end of October, and successfully prevented the town from falling into German hands before the winter weather set in.

The British and French soldiers had arrived in Ypres on the 13 October 1914. The town had great strategic importance as it blocked the way to the channel coast. Ypres was very quickly renamed 'Wipers' by the British soldiers because it was easier to pronounce, and they remained there for the next four years, up until November 1918. The civilian population remained in the town until May 1915 when they were evacuated because of the heavy German shelling of the town. Although many wanted to stay in their town, the damage to the drainage and sewerage system as well as the destruction of the buildings made it impossible for them to remain.

Ypres now appeared deserted during the day, but was actually occupied by thousands of Allied soldiers, horses and wagons, all moving about under cover of darkness. It was then that the town came alive as they made their way to and back from the front. Most soldiers preferred the winter because it extended the time they could move about in the dark. Many thousands of Allied troops died in the rubble of its ruined buildings and crater ridden farmland as they defended Ypres. Thousands more died on the way to and from the front line. The Germans carried out three major operations to retake the town in the autumn of 1914, the spring of 1915 and again in the spring of 1918. The British carried out two major offensives in 1917 to try and dislodge the Germans from the high ground which dominated the north, east and south of the town. By the end of 1918 the town was virtually completely destroyed.

Chapter 16

The Machine Gun Corps

In July 1915 the National Registration Act came in requiring every citizen between the ages of fifteen and sixty-five to register their name, marital status, where they lived and what work they were doing. The Registrar General for England, Bernard Mallet, devised quite a complicated system for a register in each local authority. In England the forms were filed first by occupational group and then alphabetically within each group. In Scotland the forms were all held in Edinburgh and filed alphabetically[1]. Emma would no doubt have joined the queue at the local registration office in Walton and filled in her form with everyone else. Once registered, she would have received a national registration card.

In October 1915, of the 21,627,596 names on the register, 5,158,211 were men who were of military age although some 1,519,432 were considered to be in reserved occupations. Men in this category had black stars against their names in official records and wore badges stating they were 'On War Service'. They also carried 'protection certificates' to stop them from being targeted with white feathers.

The 'Organization of the White Feather' was initiated by Admiral Charles Fitzgerald in August 1914. Its aim was to pressure more men to enlist in the army. Young women would hand white feathers to men who were not in uniform, the implication being they were cowards. As manpower shortages increased in 1915 so did the campaign. Even soldiers home on leave were targeted as were men who were considered to be in reserved occupations.

Conscientious objectors, those who held deep seated beliefs that war was wrong, had to appear before a tribunal. Those who refused to do anything to help with the war were normally sentenced to long spells in prison with hard labour. Others became medics or did civilian work that still aided the war, but did not involve fighting.

Despite being identified as in reserved occupations by the engineering trade union, many skilled workers still found themselves pressured into joining the forces. This left a shortfall in the number of people able to produce ships, ammunition and weapons.

The government had been relying on the pre-war factory system which could not keep pace with demand. After the 'shell shortage' row in May 1915 the Liberal Government had fallen and had been replaced with a coalition which immediately created the Ministry of Munitions. The Munitions of War Act in August 1915 bought all munitions manufacturers under this new ministry. Needing workers to replace those leaving to join the forces, the unions and employers finally agreed to accept women in their place. Although they were initially only doing unskilled work, by August 1915 they began to be accepted in roles that had previously been considered 'closed shops'. Eventually 800,000 women would be employed in factories, the majority making munitions, weapons and filling shells.

With the increase in productivity and rising prices, rumours of profiteering spread and workplace unrest increased towards the end of 1915. Strikes took place in the Clydeside shipbuilding factories during the winter of 1915/1916 and further unrest followed. For the families of those fighting and the men in the trenches, who would have been only too happy to be at home on increased wages, safe from shelling and fighting, this issue divided the nation. One estimate suggests that the 3,227 strikes involving 2.6 million workers during 1915-1918 cost 18 million working days.

Meanwhile back in Belgium in late summer 1915 things were beginning to change as it became generally accepted that machine gun specialists were urgently needed. To start with infantry machine gun sections were brigaded together under a brigade MG officer. These formed companies of sixteen guns. The Guards Division, who were one of the first to adopt the brigading system, formed four machine gun companies in September 1915. By 14 October 1915 a Royal Warrant established The Machine Gun Corps (MGC) and a training centre was set up at Belton Park in Grantham in Lincolnshire. Once trained the men would be sent to the depot and training centre in France. This had now moved to Camiers which was located a small distance from Etaples. Here they would pick up their guns and equipment and return to the units in the field.

At the time of being formed the MGC was divided into three branches. The smallest was the MGC Motors which consisted of motor cycle and sidecar combinations. The gun was fitted to the sidecar. The second was the MGC Infantry whose dedicated machine gun section would be called companies. The third was the MGC Cavalry whose machine gun sections would be called squadrons.

Throughout the winter of 1915/16 those men who were already trained in machine guns were withdrawn in rotation and sent back to Belton Camp in Grantham, Lincolnshire to receive specialist training under the tutelage of Christopher Baker-Carr. Baker-Carr, who had retired as a captain in 1905, had initially been recruited by Tom Capper[2] who had asked him to train some new machine gunners. It was his discussions with battalion commanders that led to the idea of brigading the machine gunners together as specialists rather than as separate operatives within cavalry and infantry battalions.

The Vickers machine gun had been adopted by the British in 1912[3] and had a rate of fire of 450–550 rounds per minute. Like the Lee-Enfield it used .303 ammunition. But it was water cooled and prone to jamming. It heated up very quickly, sometimes in only a couple of minutes, so it was normally fired in short sharp bursts. It would normally take four to six men to move the gun and apart from the Number 1, the man who fired the gun, they would all carry rifles.

As previously mentioned, at the beginning of the war, each infantry and cavalry battalion had its own machine gun section of two guns. But the operatives had received little training as to the real potential of the weapons, many of which were knocked out before they could be used to best advantage. Once the guns were gone that was it. There were no replacements available.

The MG Section was brigaded into the 9th Cavalry MG Squadron on 28 February 1916. But Bert did not leave the 19th Hussars to become a member of the Machine Gun Corps until 27 June 1916. Together with sixty-nine other men of the 19th Hussars Bert was compulsorily transferred to the MGC Cavalry and given the new army number 50720. It was here he met the man who was to become his best friend. 50773 Private Francis H Burke was an Australian from Queensland who had won the Distinguished

Conduct Medal for his actions in 1916. He and Bert took an instant liking to each other, found they had plenty in common and were delighted to find themselves in the same squadron.

To start with many gunners returned to the regiments they had served with, thus they were still with many of their old friends, but as time went on their deployment became much more fragmentary. In line with this 9th Squadron became the machine gun section supporting the 15th and 19th Hussars and the 1/1 Bedfordshire Yeomanry, all of whom were part of the 1st Cavalry Division.

Each machine gun team consisted of six men. The No. 1, normally an L/Cpl or Cpl, carried the tripod into action which was the heaviest part of the weapon, around 48lbs. The man who fired it was the man who selected the best site for the particular job and he looked after the mounting. No. 2 carried the gun itself which weighed around 42lbs when full of seven and a half pints of water. Nos. 3 and 4 were ammunition carriers, No. 5 was the scout while No. 6 was the range taker. Ammunition was very heavy. A single round of .303 weighed just under 1oz. The maximum rate of fire was 600 rpm which meant it could fire 33lbs of ammunition every minute. The normal sustainable rate of fire was 250rpm which was the equivalent of one belt per minute. Even at this reduced rate of fire the gun could use 15,000 rounds per minute which weighed a staggering third of a ton. The weight of the ammunition needed to keep all sixteen guns in use was about five tons per hour.

Up to thirty men from each battalion would be charged with keeping the ammunition feeding the guns which in a Division could lead to up to 1,000 men tied up just keeping ammunition flowing. The guns were water cooled and the water was stored in the barrel jackets. If the gun was firing constantly the water would very quickly rise to boiling point. The steam would leave the jacket, travel down a hose to a condensing tin where it quickly turned back into boiling water which would return to the cooling jacket. When water ran out urine would be collected and used.

Once back in Flanders Bert and Francis found themselves spending rather a lot of time in reserve as they waited for a significant break through the German lines that would allow the cavalry to exploit the large open spaces. It was as reserves to X1V Corps that they found themselves in the Battle of Fleur-Courcelette on the 15 September 1916. It was in this battle that tanks were introduced for the first time.

The attack was along a twelve mile front on the 15 September, twelve divisions took part with all forty-nine tanks, which were all the British had at that time. The early tanks weighed twenty-eight tons and could only move at a half mile per hour. Although they protected the crew against small arms fire, machine gun fire caused metal chips to fly around inside the tank. The crew were offered chain mail visors, but these were uncomfortable so rarely worn. They had no defence against shell fire which easily destroyed them. Visibility was poor, as was navigation and more than one tank found itself firing on its own troops. Because radio communication was not available at the time carrier pigeons were used instead.

The attack began with an artillery bombardment designed to leave lanes unshelled for the advance of the tanks. This meant some German strong points were untouched by the barrage. The tanks began to move forward to the line on the 11 September. Seventeen tanks broke down on the way, seven failed to start when they were due to move off. This left only twenty-five which were capable of advancing into no-man's-land on the 15 Septemeber.

As the battle raged there were several occasions when it looked as if Bert and the rest of 1st Cavalry Division would be called in to support XIV Corps who were on the right of the line and not having a very successful time. The 56th Division on the right flank had soon found themselves bogged down. On their left the 6th Division had been unable to overcome the strong German position known as the Quadrilateral, north of Leuze Wood. They had needed to do this before attacking their first objective, but despite heavy fighting, they had made little progress. The Guards Division had eventually reached their first objective, but once there they believed they were at their third objective and halted.

The offensive began again on the 16 September but made little progress and although another offensive was planned for the 17 September a combination of bad weather and German reinforcements, caused it to be postponed until the 21st. It was then cancelled.

The main affect of the launch of tanks was on local German morale as the BEF and the Canadian Corps gained just over a mile in the first three days, taking the villages of Martinpuich, Flers, Courcelette and High Wood. Although the use of tanks had not really made that much difference Haig was impressed and ordered 1,000 more to be built.

Back in reserve Bert and Francis had lived to survive another day and as the rains began again they prepared for yet another cold wet winter in

Flanders. Both of them, like all of their friends, were longing to go home. It seemed as if the war would never end and Bert despaired of ever seeing his mother again. It was a year since he'd last seen her and his leave had been only two weeks, crammed in whilst home for retraining. But those two weeks had reminded him of what it was like to be away from the war and for the first time since childhood he found himself wishing he wasn't a soldier. He was also shocked by how much Emma had aged while he had been away. He knew she worried about him and he did his best to reassure her, but he knew she didn't really believe him when he said that he spent most of his time in reserve. He also found it impossible to accurately describe conditions in Flanders, instead resorting to generalities, rather like the newspapers. It was clear that the civilians still had no real idea of the number of casualties and Bert couldn't add to his mother's worry by trying to tell her.

They had walked along the promenade several times. Listening to the waves crashing on the shore had been strangely relaxing. But even the waves couldn't drown out the intermittent sound of the guns firing across the other side of the channel, an ever present reminder that soon he would have to go back.

Since his return she had written regularly, her letters telling him what was happening at home. But to Bert it all seemed so distant now, rather like another world.

Rumours had started to reach the front that there was a lack of available or affordable food at home. For Bert, used to the shortages of their rations, this seemed rather unimportant although he was concerned that his mother was not eating enough. He had thought she looked thinner when he'd been home, but hadn't given it a lot of thought. They had eaten well while he was there so he was troubled that perhaps she had used all her food to feed him. The fact that she only seemed to mention good things and never mentioned the lack of food was also strange. He began to worry about what else she was not telling him.

The German Navy had a large fleet of U-boats and they soon realized that the best use of their submarine fleet was to sink merchant shipping bringing food and other supplies to Britain. Up until 1916 there had been no control over food, despite the fact that Britain was sixty per cent reliant on imports. At the beginning of the war there had been widespread hoarding and, as more and more shipping was targeted by the Germans, food prices rose. Most commodities rose by about fifty per cent, during the course of the war. But others rose considerably more. Fresh meat rose by a hundred per cent, fish by 200 per cent, sugar by 250 per cent and eggs by 400 per cent. In December 1916 the Ministry of Food was set up. This was mainly because of concerns about hoarding and profiteering, rather than the U-boat menace. It replaced the Cabinet Committee on Food Supplies, created in 1914 to ensure the supply of essential foods.

Seventy per cent of British sugar came from either sugar beet in Germany or Austria or sugar cane from the colonies. It was the first food item to be rationed in July 1917 and homes were allowed half a pound of sugar a week. Meat was even more of a problem. Most meat came from the Americas making it hard to get the cheaper cuts. Meat consumption fell steadily as people began to buy fish instead. This increased the price of fish so people resorted to buying offal. Many poorer families lived on a diet of potatoes, bread and cheap margarine. Those who lived in the country often subsidized their meagre diet with dandelion leaves which they put in their sandwiches or picked the greens from turnips and swedes growing in the fields. In many households the women would not eat at all, giving their food to the children.

As the Germans tripled the number of merchant ships torpedoed without warning[4] in 1917 panic buying and hoarding began again and food committees began to clamp down on any evidence of food waste. But it was not until early 1918 that ration cards were finally introduced. Householders registered with a local supplier, handed over their ration coupon for their weekly supply of meat and fats, and the supplier was guaranteed a supply in line with the number of registered customers. Although this did not solve all the shortages it did, at least, mean that everyone had something to eat.

Chapter 17

Shortages, Unrest and More Disastrous Battles

Now part of the Cavalry Corps General HQ Reserve, Bert shivered in his greatcoat and rubbed his hands together in an attempt to get some feeling back in them. He and Francis had begun April 1917 in their winter billets near the channel coast where they were told to prepare for the next offensive. To start with the weather had been fine but it had now turned cold again with snow and heavy rain showers and squally winds, an unpleasant reminder of the winter they had just endured. The winter of 1916/1917 had been long and cold, more like the winters they were used to. But the snow and ice had taken its toll as they shivered in the trenches and spent hours scraping ice off their weapons. The muddy furrows of no-man's-land also froze solid, as did the bodies of those left where they had fallen. For the men in the front line trenches the cold did at least bring some relief from the smell of the swollen bodies as they decomposed in front of them.

Two days before the start of the attack they had finally been given their orders and they began to move forward. The move had first been scheduled for the 6 April but the French had requested a twenty-four hour delay to the operation. This meant they did not start moving until the 7 April. The 1st Cavalry Division was supporting the 1st Army and was based at Corps HQ in Croix, in the valley of Ternoise, north-west of St Pol and it was freezing cold. The good weather had been replaced with heavy snow falls which had blanketed the ground in a frozen white carpet. Even worse a blizzard had just started, covering everything in a swirling mass of frozen white flakes that stung where they hit bare flesh. It was the 9 April 1917 and the First Battle of the River Scarpe was about to start. The attack was due to start at 5.30am and Bert's main concern as they waited was to keep the machine gun free from ice so he could play his part in the forthcoming battle.

The 2nd and 3rd Cavalry Divisions were attached to the Third Army under the command of General Sir E H H Allenby. The 2nd Cavalry Division were concentrated in the Authie valley from Doulens to Auix-le-Chateau with their HQ at Wavans. The 3rd Cavalry Division were in the Canche Valley from Frevent to Conchy with their HQ in Monchel.

On the 8 April they had all moved up further to their holding positions west of Arras. Here they waited for their orders to move. Bert now found himself in Frevin-Capelle, which was six miles north-west of Arras. The 2nd Cavalry Division had moved to Pas-en-Artois, sixteen miles north-west of Arras while the 3rd was at Gouy-en-Artois, nine miles to the west.

All around them the air was filled with the deafening sound of the Allied heavy artillery as they continued their week long pounding of the enemy positions. The acrid smell of spent cordite mixed with the icy swirling snow, adding to the effects of the blizzard, and catching in the throats of the men as they waited for the orders to advance.

As the artillery stopped abruptly silence fell and then they could hear the distant cries of the infantry as they went over the top and advanced towards the German lines. Now the air was filled with the rattle of machine guns, rifle fire, shouts of encouragement and the screams of the dying. Back at HQ Bert and Francis waited impatiently with their comrades, waiting for the orders which would allow them to join the battle.

Finally, at 4pm, news began to filter back that the opening phase of the battle had been successful across the whole of the fifteen mile front. The infantry were in position, it was time for the Cavalry Corps and the 17th (Northern) Division, who were supporting them, to move southwards to their positions east of Arras. Here they would wait for the opportunity to exploit any advance towards the German Third Line which spanned both north and south of the Cambrai Road.

The 2nd and 3rd Cavalry Divisions formed up in two columns ready to move southwards. The left column consisted of the 3rd Cavalry Divisions with 50th Brigade, and 17th (Northern Division). On the right were 52nd Brigade who were supporting the 2nd Cavalry Division. The 1st Cavalry Division was a part of the Divisional Reserve and as such were kept back at HQ, much to Bert's intense frustration.

The first objective for the advancing cavalry was to establish a line along the left bank of the River Sensee and then to secure a line on the Drocourt-Quearnt Switch Line. This was an additional defensive part of the Hindenburg Line. Unfortunately the orders to move had come through so late that the left column was ordered to halt once they reached the western suburbs of Arras and find billets for the night. The right column had managed to take the German first line at Tilloy-les-Mofflaines and then progressed as far as the eastern suburbs, when they too halted for the night. Other parts of 50th Brigade found themselves camping out in a field by the side of the Arras-Cambrai road. To add to their misery heavy snow had begun to fall again covering everything in a thick, white, freezing cold, blanket that blocked out sound and left the men feeling isolated. To make matters worse, the following day the divisional attachments were removed and sent to V1 Corps.

The 2nd Cavalry Division now attempted to push south past the village of Monchy-le-Preux at the same time as the 3rd Division attempted to push north. But because the artillery was ineffective both attacks failed and the men became caught up in masses of defensive barbed wire entanglements where they were mowed down by deadly accurate machine gun fire.

But, on the 11 April at 5am, despite the heavy snow, the 37th Division, with support from the Cavalry, continued the assault. The advancing men were subject to a massive German artillery bombardment and heavy machine gun fire from the village, but still they continued to attack. At 8.30am the cavalry began their own assault. Unfortunately the artillery had again been largely ineffective against the strong German defences. To the horror of the advancing cavalry they were still virtually intact. Hours of heavy fighting followed. By 8.20pm it was obvious their position was hopeless and those who were left were ordered to fall back. The 2nd Cavalry Division fell back to the Crinchon Valley, south-west of Arras and the 3rd Division followed a more circular route to the north. Here they found billets between the St Pol road and River Scarpe and on the racecourse.

Meanwhile, Bert, Francis and the rest of the 1st Cavalry Division were still waiting impatiently in reserve at GHQ, six miles north-west of Arras at Frevin-Capelle. Realizing the support of a Cavalry Division could open additional options for him, Allenby asked for a brigade from the 1st Division to support XV11 Corps north of the River Scarpe. Haig agreed, but although 1st Cavalry Division was in GHQ Reserve, it still came under the command of Cavalry Corps which was under 3rd Army command.

The orders from GHQ went via Cavalry Corps HQ. They were telephoned through at 4.15pm, and Cavalry Corps in turn, rang 1st Division to warn them to be ready. Corps HQ then received a wire from GHQ confirming the order at 4.55pm but didn't pass it on. Having heard nothing to confirm their orders, 1st Division then sought confirmation direct from GHQ. But this wasn't received until 6.15pm. By then it was too late. The 1st Brigade was moved quickly up as far as Athies and then came to an abrupt halt. The impetus had been lost and the opportunity to make significant gains had been squandered.

Back at HQ Bert sipped his mug of tea, smoked another cigarette and tried to curb his rising frustration. He knew Francis felt the same. Despite their extra training they had still not had the opportunity to put it into practice. Yes, they had survived another battle, but they were both beginning to feel guilty that everyone was fighting but them. He looked at the letter he was writing to his mother and smiled as he re-read his moans about not being involved in the fighting. He knew his mother would be delighted that yet again he had spent the battle in reserve and he smiled. He wondered what she was doing now and whether she was thinking about him.

Back home things were getting worse. There were now considerable food shortages, especially as the cost of bread, the staple of most people's diet, had risen almost a hundred per cent by 1917.[1] The government stepped in and, by subsidizing it, fixed the price at 9d. Although there was a short period during 1917 in which there was virtually no flour, bread was never actually rationed. However, the quality rapidly deteriorated as potato flour and chalk was used instead of wheat flour. Although these did bulk up the content of the bread, it darkened the colour, roughened the texture and had a very unpleasant taste and smell. Furthermore it cost the bakers more to produce as they had to buy new equipment to boil potatoes and because it was difficult to mash, many people found themselves eating bread with lumps of potato in.

But that other staple of the British diet, potatoes, were also in such short supply in 1917 that there was a shortage of seed potatoes to plant for the following year's crop. In an attempt to prevent a crisis the food controller distributed an additional 15,000 tons of seed potatoes to allotment holders as well as farmers. The other reason for the shortages was the lack of men working on farms. Although women had been working on many farms since the beginning of the war, in 1917 the Women's Land Army was formed to ensure there was enough manpower to grow the potatoes and other crops.

There were also worries about the underlying inequalities of British society that were increasingly becoming the focus of unrest. In Russia the revolution had swept away the ruling class and there were concerns that the same thing would happen in Britain. The War Cabinet was so worried that it set up a special Commission on Industrial Unrest in April 1917 to monitor the morale of the working classes.

The country needed the co-operation and support of the working classes to continue to fight the war, but many were living in sub-standard housing. The rooms or houses they were renting from private landlords often had poor sanitation, if any, and a lack of running water. They were cold and damp in the winter, and hot and airless in the summer and often infested with vermin. Overcrowding was a major problem because of the large size of families and also because extended families lived together.

In the cities the problem grew worse because there was a sudden need to accommodate ten per cent more workers. Although the Ministry of Munitions built 12,000 homes for its workers 20,000 still ended up living in hostels, schools or church halls. Because many of these were run on similar grounds to the workhouse they were normally avoided by those they were meant for. Construction of private houses had more or less ground to a halt since the beginning of the war so private landlords began cashing in on the acute housing shortage by reopening properties that had been condemned as unfit for human habitation.

To try and alleviate the problem the government brought in the Billeting of Civilian's Act in the spring of 1918. Local authorities now had the power to make homeowners let out their spare rooms at a fixed price. Whilst many objected, others were only too pleased to make some extra money. Unscrupulous landlords had also imposed huge rent rises which eventually led to strikes and even more unrest. One of the reasons behind the Clydeside ship strike was the massive increase in rents. Seriously worried about production levels the government rushed through the Rent Restriction Act. This pushed rents back down to their pre-war level and held them there. Although this was a success for the tenants, many landlords now claimed they could not afford to provide any repairs or maintenance.

Others just ignored the ruling, raised rents anyway and evicted those who couldn't pay.

One of the biggest problems caused by poor housing was ill health. In July 1917 the Bishop of London stated although nine soldiers were killed per hour in 1915, the mortality rate for babies was even higher with twelve babies dying every hour. With increased death rates from the war the number of births began to decline. In an attempt to stem this infant welfare centres were set up and the number of midwives and full time health visitors increased. As the war progressed the infant death rate gradually began to decline.

Because letters from Britain weren't censored news soon filtered through to the men in the trenches about the housing problems. Even worse though was the coal shortage. The first few months of 1917 was one of the coldest on record and the year as a whole was also colder than normal. Coal fires were the principle source of heating and prices had risen dramatically since the beginning of the war. There were also shortages and the supply was intermittent. These were caused by labour shortages because many miners had joined the army and because of increased industrial demand. Many shops began closing early to save on the cost of heating and lighting and families went to bed earlier to try and save money.

The shortage was so acute by 1917 that the police were called in to stop rioting at railway distribution centres and children were sent out to collect sticks and other wood from parks and open spaces to supplement the fuel supply. By October the authorities had no option but to introduce coal rationing in London. For the working class this meant they would have equal access to coal. As the poor only had small rooms they were considerably warmer than their middle class and upper class counter parts. They were only entitled to the same amount of coal as the poor so they were unable to heat all their rooms and their rooms were often bigger.

Back in France the men were seriously concerned about their families back home and many complained to the padres who passed their concerns back up the chain of command. But eventually news from home began to take second place as the men prepared to move to their next battle, that of Passchendale.

Chapter 18

Cambrai

After a long trek from their billets in Roclincourt and Ecurie camp Bert and Francis arrived in Peronne in November 1917. They had spent the summer with the rest of the brigade at Vimy Ridge reinforcing communication trenches and digging new ones. Although the work was hard it was also strangely satisfying. For once the weather was good and they had plenty of rations although the water did taste rather strange. Even better they were away from the chaos and destruction of the front line so in the evenings they were able to really relax. Playing cards, singing songs, telling stories, holding concert parties, beer from the canteen, all made their time the most enjoyable since they'd arrived in Europe so many years ago.

New songs were now dong the rounds. *The Old French Trench* was a new favourite.

'*Oh what a life, living in a trench, Under Johnny French in the old French Trench, We haven't got a wife or a nice little wench, But we're still alive in the old French trench.*'

Followed by one of the most popular ones *I don't want to die*.

'*I want to go home, I want to go home, I don't want to go in the trenches no more, Where whizz bangs and shrapnel they whistle and roar, take me over the sea, Where the alley man can't get me, Oh my, I don't want to die, I want to go home.*'

It wasn't all fun as some nights they would continue digging the communication trenches under cover of darkness. Other nights they had training which often meant route marches along tracks with quaintly sounding names given to them by the men. The Duckboard track, Ouse Valley, Oppy Switch, Tired Alley and Essex Walk were just some of the names of the tracks the men used, returning exhausted to their billets at two or three in the morning.

Having finally adjusted to life away from the front line Bert was disappointed to find dozens of lorries lined up at Labyrinth Avenue one evening. It was time to return to their horses and get ready for the next battle in which the cavalry was to be used. It was time to go to Passchendale. Bert, Francis and the rest of 9th Squadron MGC packed up their gun and joined the rest of the cavalry as they moved up to Dickebusch. Here they stayed for a few days and then, to their utmost astonishment, they were sent back to the same camps they had left only a few days earlier. With much grumbling the men unpacked again only to be told they were going to be involved in the next offensive to take Cambrai.

After being told the day of the assault the officers and NCOs were given their instructions. New maps were issued, the colour of the very lights and streamers were explained and they were also told about the types of aeroplanes that would be supporting them.

Just before midnight on the 19 November, they began the long walk to their positions. It was pitch black and the men could see very little. Their initial order was to march at ease, but they were not allowed to smoke. As they came closer they were given the order to stop talking. From then on all that could be heard was the sound of the horses clipping along the ground, the creaking of saddles and the odd dull clanging sound of the bridles. Occasionally someone coughed, the sound muffled in the darkness as the men carried on through the cold, damp, winter's night. They arrived at Fins at about 3am and unsaddled the horses. Now was the worst time, the time before zero hour, which in this case, was set for 6am.

As the false dawn began to slowly light the sky some of the men were detailed onto fodder fatigue. Bert looked around him in amazement. The area was filled with all the cavalry that was in France at that time. As he gazed around he spotted some of the men he'd met over the years and nudging Francis he pointed out people he'd never expected to see again. Neither he, nor Francis, had seen so many horses and men all together in one place. It seemed every regiment was represented, Dragoons, Lancers, Hussars, even the Indian mounted troops.

The first Battle of Cambrai began on the 20 November 1917 at 6.20am. At the time the Italian forces were about to be overrun and were suffering heavy casualties so Haig attempted to divert some of the German forces away from them. There was no artillery bombardment before the attack as it was hoped the element of surprise would be enough for the troops to overrun the German trenches. The idea was for the tanks to break through the barbed wire entanglements and open the way for the cavalry to charge through the gaps.

The front extended from Havrincourt to La Vacquerie, a total of six miles, which on the morning of the attack was shrouded in mist. As the infantry and tanks advanced towards the Germans 1,000 British guns began a creeping barrage. Many Germans fled in panic when they saw that the tanks had managed to cross the Hindenburg Line, but at Havrincourt, Ribecourt and Flesquires there was heavy fighting as the Germans dug in and refused to give ground. Despite the infantry's inexperience of working with tanks the first two villages were eventually taken. But at Flesquires the approach was a long slope manned by German machine gunners. The 1st Cavalry Division had advanced under the mistaken impression that the village had already fallen. The defending Germans fought hard putting several tanks out of action and the Division took heavy casualties.

The Indian mounted troops left first. By now the creeping barrage had started and was already getting heavier. Rumours reached the men that the tanks and infantry had taken the Hindenburg trenches and as they waited they saw prisoners coming towards them. This was a good sign and Bert's spirits rose. Then it was their turn to move, crossing the Hindenburg line easily, past the burnt out tanks and bodies of dead infantry, eyes ahead waiting for any sign of the enemy.

To Bert it seemed like they were marching for hours, the only Germans they saw were prisoners. Then, in the afternoon, they were bought up short by an artillery barrage. This caused some casualties, including two of the horses who had to be destroyed. Having rapidly taken cover behind a hedge Bert, Francis and the rest of the men set up their machine gun and began firing back until they were given the order to withdraw.

The rest of the afternoon was spent moving around until it began raining heavily, soaking them and eventually trickling through their puttees.

Finding an open field they stood patiently with the horses waiting for orders. At midnight they were told to unsaddle the horses and bed down for the night. Sleeping in the wet fields was not a prospect that pleased anyone, but having no choice they did as they were told and tried to get some sleep.

Meanwhile the tanks had managed to capture the bridge at Marcoing before it could be destroyed, but at Masnieres the bridge was too badly damaged for the tanks to cross the Schelde Canal, something they needed to do to advance against Cambrai. But their fire power enabled the infantry to cross and by the end of the day they had taken all three Hindenburg trenches, captured Graincourt, Marcoing and Mesnieres and cut off Flesquieres from support. In all they had advanced 10,000 yards. But although the tanks had managed to push forward into Bourlon Wood the infantry were now too tired to follow.

Back in the open field it was gone midnight and Bert and Francis were doing their best to get some rest. But this was interrupted by the arrival of some of the men who had been woken and sent to pick up the ammunition for the machine guns which had been dumped further down the road. As this would be needed by Bert, Francis and their colleagues the next day, there were no complaints, only relief that they would be able to do the job they had trained so hard for.

The morning broke damp, wet and misty and the men had their bully beef breakfast. Like the cavalry who were tired from lack of sleep, the infantry too were exhausted and the tanks had already survived one major engagement, but the battle continued unabated. The Allies gradually closed up on the east of Cambrai, taking 500 prisoners at Cantaing. But when the 1st Division finally received orders to advance to Cantaing the Germans had used the intervening two hours to reoccupy it. They were met with heavy machine gun fire and forced to withdraw.

Early in the afternoon the tanks and some squadrons of the 1st Cavalry Division stormed Fontaine-Notre-Dame. As they advanced they came under fire from the air as enemy planes began bombing them mercilessly. The village was still some distance away and as the cavalry galloped towards it Bert, Francis and the machine guns provided covering fire. The machine gun fire was so intense that the Germans were unable to bring their own four machine guns into play and the teams manning them stayed in their dugouts throughout the whole attack.

Once in the village though fierce hand-to-hand fighting took place as some of the the Germans climbed out of their dugouts and began throwing bombs while others surrendered. Although they took several prisoners the Germans began counter attacking with machine guns and artillery. Towards midnight the shelling died down, but the next day the Germans continued their counter attack and retook the village.

By the 23 November virtually all of Bourlon Woods was in the hands of the Allies, but the Germans were now bringing up masses of reserves through the large railway junction at Cambrai. This effectively prevented the Allies from taking Bourlon village and retaking Fontaine-Notre-Dame. Both tank crews and infantry had fought to a standstill and were completely exhausted. They were also facing fresh troops as the Germans continued to flood the area with reserves. But, despite this, efforts to retake the villages continued up until the 27 November.

Eventually the cavalry were told to take their horses further back out of range. They were joined at around midnight by the infantry and they made their way wearily back to Metz. They arrived at about 3am, watered and fed the horses and then tried to grab some sleep before reveille at 6am. It was only as they collected their rations that the true number of casualties really struck them. The rations had come up for a full regiment, but now, instead of three or four to a loaf of bread, it was just two per loaf. The rain continued and the men found themselves knee-deep in mud yet again. Rumours flew round saying they were to be to be used as dismounted troops, but no order came. Then, at 11pm, just as the men began to relax and doze off, the order came to fall in.

Completely exhausted, the men had trouble rousing themselves, but nevertheless they fell in and awaited their next orders. As they stood in the pouring rain they were a strange sight with their blankets and rolled ground sheets worn bandolier fashion over their ammunition belts. Unlike the infantry they did not have packs.

Haig's plan had always been to take the high ground of Bourlon Wood and to use his cavalry to isolate Cambrai. But by the 30 November the Germans had brought in heavy reinforcements from the Eastern Front and the victory had been lost.

Chapter 19

The Spring Offensive

Emma glanced at the headlines of the newspapers as she walked past the shops. Despite several skirmishes during the winter many had continued to carry the headlines 'All quiet on the Western Front'. But by the beginning of 1918 the tone had changed and several newspapers began to carry reports that the Germans were building up to a Spring Offensive. Back on the Home Front the majority of the population still did not recognize the seriousness of the threat about to face the Allies. Despite years of casualties a kind of battle fatigue had crept in. Many no longer believed the eyewitness accounts from journalists and most still thought the Allies would win, especially now the USA had entered the war. Others thought it was some kind of ploy to ensure more reserves were sent to the front as the War Cabinet had ordered Haig to take over the French Front in January, but Lloyd George and Robertson had decided to limit the number of reserves being sent to France.

Emma had no idea what to believe anymore. She had not seen Bert for two years[1] and although she received letters from him on a regular basis her instincts told her that he was not telling her everything. Leave for the average soldier throughout the war was sporadic. Although officers came home regularly the men came home only once a year, if they were lucky. Travelling time would not be taken into consideration and would come out of the time allocated. Most arrived home in full kit with many still covered in mud from the battlefield.

Over six inches of snow had fallen during the night of the 16 January only to be followed the following night by torrential rain. At least the rain had washed away the snow and the temperature had risen which helped preserve

SAW 035866

CERTIFIED COPY OF   **ENTRY OF DEATH**

Application Number 32 8 5039/1

Registration of Births, Deaths and   **Marriages (Special Provisions) Act 1957**

Return of Warrant Officers, Non-Commissioned Officers and Men of the Machine Gun Corps. (Cavalry)
Killed in Action or who have died whilst on Service Abroad in the War of 1914 to 1921

Regt. or Army number	Rank	Name in Full (Surname First)	Age	Country of Birth	Date of Death	Place of Death	Cause of Death
50720	Pte.	COLUMBINE Herbert George	26	England	22.3.1918	France	Killed in Action

An Entry relating to the death of Herbert George Columbine

CERTIFIED to be a true copy of the *certified copy of* an entry in a Service Departments Register.
Given at the General Register office, under the seal of the said Office, the 30th day of June 2011

Section 3(2) of the above mentioned Act provides that "The enactments relating to the registration of births and deaths and marriages in England and Wales, Scotland
and Northern Ireland (which contain provisions authorising the admission in evidence of, and of extracts from, certified copies of registers and duplicate registers) shall
If the certificate is have effect as if the Service Departments Registers were certified copies or duplicate registers transmitted to the Registrar General in accordance with those enactments."
given from the original
Register the words "the CAUTION: THERE ARE OFFENCES RELATING TO FALSIFYING OR ALTERING A CERTIFICATE AND USING OR POSSESSING A FALSE CERTIFICATE. © Crown Copyright
certified copy of" are
struck out. WARNING: A CERTIFICATE IS NOT EVIDENCE OF IDENTITY

Herbert's death certificate.

her meagre coal stocks. But as January and February gave way to March the weather improved considerably and on the 9 March the Germans began intermittent shelling of the British lines. Many of the long-range shells landed a long way behind the front line leading the papers to state the shelling was futile. However, this was all part of the German plan to disrupt communication lines so that when the offensive began the front line would not be able to communicate with the military authorities in the rear.

As she went shopping on the 22 March Emma saw that several of the papers were now carrying news that the expected German Spring Offensive had started the day before. Quickly scanning the page she read that there would be plenty of hard fighting before it was over and her spirits fell. Bert had survived so long she found it hard to believe his luck would continue to hold, but believe she must so she sighed and went to join the queues for food. Since 1917 the Germans had been blockading the channel preventing food and other supplies getting through. Eventually rationing had been introduced but despite this food was becoming more and more expensive and harder to get hold of. She was grateful that she only had to feed herself

AncestryLibrary.com - UK, Soldiers Died in the Great War, 1914-1919 | Page 1 of 1

ENQ NO: 182352

ancestry library edition

UK, Soldiers Died in the Great War, 1914-1919

Name:	**Herbert George Colombine**
Birth Place:	Chelsca, Middx.
Residence:	Walton-On-Naze, Essex
Death Date:	22 Mar 1918
Death Location:	France & Flanders
Enlistment Location:	Colchester, Essex
Rank:	Private
Regiment:	Machine Gun Corps
Battalion:	(Cavalry)
Number:	50720
Type of Casualty:	Killed in action
Theatre of War:	Western European Theatre
Comments:	Vc., Formerly 5780, 19Th Hussars.

Source Information:
Military-Genealogy.com, comp. *UK, Soldiers Died in the Great War, 1914-1919* [database on-line]. Provo, UT, USA: Ancestry.com Operations Inc, 2008.
Original data: *British and Irish Military Databases*. The Naval and Military Press Ltd.

Description:
This database contains information extracted from 81 volumes of soldiers that died in World War I. It includes over 703,000 individuals. Information listed about may include: name of soldier, birthplace, enlistment place, residence, number, decoraton, rank, regiment, battalion, type of casualty, death date, death place, and theater of war served in.

© 2011, The Generations Network, Inc.

Herbert's death registered as one of the UK soldiers who died in the Great War.

and she pitied the poor mothers with numerous children. Even with the introduction of free school meals in 1914 it must still be a struggle. Fortunately living by the coast meant there was invariable some extra fish to be had so her diet now was predominately based on fish. As she stood in the queue waiting her turn, her mind wandered back to Bertie and she wondered what he was doing and if he was safe.

Bert and Francis had spent the winter in the rear of the lines preparing for the Spring Offensive which everyone in France knew was coming. The priority of the British over the winter of 1917/1918 had been to repair the roads and construct new supply lines, hospitals and light railways, as well as

Mrs. Columbine : Awarded to her son, the late No. 50720 Private Herbert George COLUMBINE, Machine Gun Corps.

For most conspicuous bravery and self-sacrifice when, owing to casualties, Private Columbine took over command of a gun and kept it firing from 9 a.m. till 1 p.m. in an isolated position with no wire in front. During this time wave after wave of the enemy failed to get up to him. Owing to his being attacked by a low-flying aeroplane the enemy at last gained a strong footing in the trench on either side. The position being untenable he ordered the two remaining men to get away, and, though being bombed from either side, kept his gun firing and inflicting tremendous losses. He was eventually killed by a bomb, which blew up him and his gun. He showed throughout the highest valour, determination, and self-sacrifice.

The Times: Monday, June 24th, 1918

A notice in *The Times* of June 24th 1918 on the day Emma went to pick up her son's posthumous VC.

digging more trenches and installing more barbed wire opposite the Hindenberg Line. As they had spent the last two years attacking the Germans many of their positions were temporary rather than permanent. The army also lacked training in how to defend effectively.

However, now that America had entered the war, the Germans needed to take decisive action before the Americans could flood the Western Front with men and equipment. The perfect opportunity came when the Russians withdrew from the war after the Russian Revolution. This allowed the Germans to transfer all their troops on the Eastern Front across to the west. The Germans devised a plan, codenamed Michael, to split the British and French Armies and capture the Channel Ports to prevent reinforcements landing. The attack was aimed towards Amiens, where the British southern flank joined with the French northern flank. Because they expected the British to draw reserves from Flanders a second attack, codenamed George, would take place near Hazebrouck and then break through to the Channel.

The Germans had also developed a new type of attack. Specially trained storm troopers would lead the assault. This would take place after a short artillery bombardment followed by the use of poison gas. Storm troopers carried little with them other than their weaponry, including flame

British Army WWI Medal Rolls Index Cards, 1914-1920 record for Herbert Columbine

Record Index

Name: Herbert Columbine

Regiment or Corps: 19th Hussars, Machine Gun Corps (Cavalry)

Source Information

A copy of Herbert's medal registered on the WW1 Medal Rolls Card Index.

COLUMBINE, HERBERT GEORGE, Private, No. 50720, was born on the 28th Nov. 1893, in London, son of Herbert Columbine (killed in action on the 11th July, 1900, in South Africa), and Emma Columbine. He was educated at Melvin Road Council Schools, Penge, and joined the Army in 1911, as a Private in the 19th Hussars, and later transferred to the Machine Gun Corps. He served in the European War in France from Aug. 1914, being killed in action 22 March, 1918. He was awarded the Victoria Cross [London Gazette, 3 May, 1918] : " Herbert George Columbine, No. 50720, Private, 9th Squadron, Machine Gun Corps. For most conspicuous bravery and self-sacrifice displayed when, owing to casualties, Private Columbine took over command of a gun and kept it firing from 9 a.m. till 1 p.m. in an isolated position with no wire in front. During this time wave after wave of the enemy failed to get up to him. Owing to his being attacked by a low-flying aeroplane, the enemy at last gained a strong footing in the trench on either side. The position being untenable, he ordered the two remaining men to get away, and, though being bombed from either side, he kept his gun firing and inflicted tremendous losses. He was eventually killed by a bomb which blew up him and his gun. He showed throughout the highest valour, determination and self-sacrifice."

Herbert G. Columbine.

The deed is thus described by Dr. P. G. C. Atkinson, who was an eye-witness :

" Nothing I have seen or heard of could be finer than the heroism of this soldier. The enemy attacked suddenly in great force. They made considerable headway, and from 'vantage ground on either side they started to enfilade our trenches, causing very severe casualties among the men. Part of our defence system included a machine-gun post somewhat in advance of the main trench. The men working this were all knocked out. Running the gauntlet of very heavy fire, Private Columbine rushed forward and took charge of this gun. He was followed by some comrades, and, in spite of the fact that the whole of the enemy machine guns in the immediate neighbourhood concentrated their heaviest fire against the post, which was almost unprotected by any of the devices commonly used, Columbine kept the machine gun going for over four hours. All that time the comrades were working round the position with strong forces, and actually had the post cut off save for one narrow gap, by which it was still possible to communicate with the main position. For the whole of the time, save when he went across the fire-swept ground to bring ammunition, the brave chap remained at his post, and, despite repeated rushes, he kept the enemy at bay. In the course of the fight a German officer appeared and repeatedly urged his men to the attack on the isolated post, but every rush of the Germans was stopped in a few yards by the deadly fire from this brave gunner, who was actually wounded, but continued to work his gun in spite of that. Early in the afternoon it became obvious that the position was hopeless, and Columbine told the only two unwounded comrades left that it was folly for them to remain

there. ' Save yourselves ; I'll carry on,' was what he said. They were reluctant to go, but he insisted, and in the end they came to see the force of his contention that there was no point in sacrificing three lives where one was enough. He shouted a few words of farewell, and that was the last his comrades heard from him. From where we lay we could see the fight going on, the swarms of grey-blue infantry around the position, the machine gun, manned by the wounded hero, spitting out death. In the course of the hour, from noon to one, the enemy made eight attempts to rush the post. Each one was brought to a standstill. Therefore new tactics were necessary. Retiring to their position the enemy concentrated heavy rifle and machine-gun fire on the hero and his gun. At the same time a number of hostile aeroplanes appeared overhead. They were promptly engaged by our machines, but one detached itself from the fighting group and came down to about a hundred feet or so above the machine-gun position, circling above for a few seconds like a great vulture ready to pounce on its prey. We saw Columbine elevate his gun to attack his new enemy. The fight could only have one ending. A bomb was launched from the aeroplane, and there was a sharp report, gun and gunner blown up. The heroic fight of Columbine was not without its value, for the way in which he delayed the enemy attack gave us time to consolidate our position in the immediate neighbourhood, and when the enemy attacked they found that the four hours' stand made by this one man had put the German plans hopelessly out of gear so far as the capture of that series of positions was concerned. The comrades of the dead hero speak highly of him."

In a letter to the deceased soldier's mother, Capt. MacAndrews, commanding the 9th Machine Gun Squadron, wrote :

" The news reached this Brigade last night that the King has the pleasure of granting your son the Victoria Cross. He nobly earned the honour, his bravery and determination on 22 March are beyond words. This is the only V.C. which this Brigade has had ; in fact, I think it is the only one the Division has had. I had a full parade of the Squadron this morning to read out the account of his action and also the letter of congratulation which we received from the General ' on behalf of the whole Brigade on the bestowal of this very distinguished honour.' In your loss of such a gallant son you have the very deepest sympathy of everyone in this Squadron, where he used to be so extremely popular. We all sincerely trust that your great sorrow may be to some extent lessened by your pride of his noble death, so noble that the King has honoured him with the very highest award."

Lieut. Eade, 9th Machine Gun Squadron, wrote :

" You will no doubt have been informed by the War Office that No. 50720, Private Columbine, H. G., is wounded and missing. He was in my sub-section, and although I had not the luck to be with him on the 22nd March, I heard what happened from those who were. He kept his gun firing to the last, although the Germans had got into the trench on 'bo'i sides of him and were throwing bombs at him. In the end he was seen to be hit by a bomb and very badly wounded. He was one of my best gun numbers, and is a great loss to the squadron. I deeply sympathize with you, but it may be some consolation to you to know that he has been recommended for a medal in token of his bravery. It was the bravest deed I have ever heard of."

Press coverage of Herbert's VC.

throwers. This meant they were not weighted down with lots of equipment. Their orders were to bypass any pockets of resistance and when they reviewed the strategy for the following day reserves would be sent to where the attack was succeeding, not where it had stalled. Thus any objectives for the following day would be set from what had been achieved that day.

It wasn't only attack methods that had changed. Defensive tactics had also undergone changes. Instead of fully manning the front line trenches only a few men occupied them. They were protected by barbed wire entanglements and strong redoubts with machine guns. They would hold off the attacker while the main defence force, who were dug in on the reverse slope, prepared for the assault. Then the artillery would begin shelling the attackers.

The Allies had been expecting a German offensive once winter had passed. They knew it would take place before the arrival of fully trained American soldiers, something that was not expected until the spring of 1918 at the earliest. But despite a number of trench raids made on the German

"East Anglian Daily Times",
1918.

ESSEX V.C. HERO'S STAND.

"SAVE YOURSELVES: I'LL CARRY ON."

This war has provided no finer act of heroic self-sacrifice than that to the credit of Pte. Columbine, a Walton-on-the-Naze Machine-gunner, whose name appears in the latest list of V.C.'s. The deed which won for this hero the Cross at he cost of his life is thus described by Dr. P. G. C. Atkinson, who was an eye-witness:—

"Nothing I have seen or heard of could be finer than the heroism of this soldier. The enemy attacked suddenly in great force. They made considerable headway, and from vantage ground on either side they started to enfilade our trenches, causing very severe casualties among the men. Part of our defence system included a machine-gun post somewhat in advance of the main trench. The men working this were all knocked out. Running the gauntlet of very heavy fire, Pte. Columbine rushed forward and took charge of this gun. He was followed by some comrades, and in spite of the fact that the whole of the enemy machine-guns in the immediate neighbourhood concentrated their heaviest fire against the post, which was almost unprotected by any of the devices commonly used, Columbine kept the machine-gun going for over four hours. All that time the enemy had been working round the position with strong forces, and actually had the post cut off save for one narrow gap, by which it was still possible to communicate with the main position. For the whole of the time, save when he went across the fire-swept ground to bring ammunition, the brave chap remained at his post, and, despite repeated rushes, he kept the enemy at bay.

"In the course of the fight a German officer appeared and repeatedly urged his men to the attack on the isolated post, but every rush of the Germans was stopped in a few yards by the deadly fire from this brave gunner, who was actually wounded, but continued to work his gun in spite of that. Early in the afternoon it became obvious that the position was hopeless, and Columbine told the only two unwounded comrades left that it was folly for them to remain there. 'Save yourselves; I'll carry on,' was what he said. They were reluctant to go, but he insisted; and in the end they came to see the force of his contention that there was no point in sacrificing three lives where one was enough. He shouted a few words of farewell, and that was the last his comrades heard from him. From where we lay we could see the fight going on, the swarms of grey-blue infantry around the position, and the machine-gun, manned by the wounded hero, spitting out death. In the course of the hour, from noon to one, the enemy made eight attempts to rush the post. Each one was brought to a standstill. Therefore new tactics were necessary.

"Retiring to their positions the enemy concentrated heavy rifle and machine-gun fire on the hero and his gun. At the same time a number of hostile aeroplanes appeared overhead. They were promptly engaged by our machines, but one detached itself from the fighting group and came down to about a hundred feet or so above the machine-gun position, circling about for a few seconds like a great vulture ready to pounce on its prey. We saw Columbine elevate his gun to attack this new enemy. The fight could only have one ending. A bomb was launched from the aeroplane, and there was a sharp report, gun and gunner being blown up. The heroic fight of Columbine was not without its value, for the way in which he delayed the enemy's attack gave us time to consolidate our position in the immediate neighbourhood, and when the enemy attacked they found that the four hours' stand made by this one man had put the German plans hopelessly out of gear so far as the capture of that series of positions was concerned. The comrades of the dead hero speak highly of him."

Local press coverage of Herbert's VC.

NAMES OF VC HOLDERS ON MEMORIALS IN FRANCE

Pozieres Memorial   Villers-Bretonneux Memorial (Somme)   Vimy Memorial   Vis-en-Artois Memorial

POZIERES MEMORIAL, FRANCE

Name	Herbert George, COLUMBINE	Edmund, DE WIND	Wilfrith, ELSTOB	
Rank	Private	2nd Lieutenant	Lieutenant Colonel	
Force	9th Squadron, Machine Gun Corps	15th Bn, Royal Irish Rifles	Comd 16th Bn, Manchester Regiment	
VC won	Hervilly Wood, France, 22 March 1918	Groagie, France, 21 March 1918	St Quentin, France, 21 March 1918	
London Gaz	28 June 1918	15 May 1919	9 June 1919	
Born	Penge, London, 28 November 1893	Comber, Co Down, 11 December 1883	Chichester, Sussex, 8 September 1888	
Died	22 March 1918, Hervilly Wood, France	21 March 1918, Groagie, France	21 March 1918, St Quentin, France	
Grave	No known grave Name on the Pozieres Memorial	No known grave Name on the Pozieres Memorial	No known grave Name on the Pozieres Memorial	
Location of VC	Royal British Legion, Walton on Naze, Essex	Not publicly held	Manchester Regiment Museum, Ashton under Lyne	
Remarks	None	None	None	

Names of VC holders on memorials in France showing Herbert Columbine.

positions on the 19 and 20 March, little information was gained, and they still had no idea where the attack would come. Although Haig was concerned that the Germans would try to seize the Channel Ports the Government would not give him any more troops. This left him with no option but to take troops from the south of his command and move them to the Channel. This left the area around St Quentin dangerously undermanned. Furthermore the trench system had not been completed and those that had been dug were inadequate.

Over a number of nights the Germans moved another 500,000 men into position. By Thursday, 21 March 1918 they had seventy-six divisions along a fifty mile front in the St Quentin area compared to only twenty-eight Allied divisions, a total of 200,000 men.

At 4.35am, on a foggy morning, with visibility down to ten yards in places, the German offensive began. One million one hundred and sixty shells fell over an 80km front in a five hour period, making it the largest

The Deathless Story of

AN

ESSEX V.C.

(Pte. H. G. COLUMBINE, Machine Gun Corps,

OF   WALTON-ON-THE-NAZE).

✠ ✠ ✠

Read it carefully and then respond to the appeal at the end as your conscience shall bid you and your pride and gratitude impel you.

Price 2d.

Weston & Dawson, Walton & Frinton

The collection for a memorial to Herbert begins.

bombardment ever seen. The Germans used 6,473 artillery guns and 3,532 mortars and over 3,000 shells fell every minute. They fell simultaneously on both the front and rear positions of the British and included every weapon available, including poison gas. While mustard and chlorine gas, trench mortars, tear gas and smoke canisters were aimed at the forward trenches, heavy artillery shelled the rear positions. These destroyed British artillery and supply lines. Communication lines were soon in chaos with telephone lines cut by the artillery bombardment and runners unable to find their way through the combination of heavy shelling and dense fog. This meant that forward positions couldn't communicate with battalion and divisional headquarters and there was no communication with the artillery.

The inadequate trenches collapsed, men were blown apart, others left stunned by the force of the onslaught. Some were lucky enough to be rendered unconscious by the noxious fumes from the gas shells, before dying. Other were left vomiting, coughing, or were blinded. Machine-gun posts were blown sky high along with their operators. Everywhere along the front the men tried desperately to hold their positions. And still the barrage continued.

Programme for the unveiling ceremony of the memorial.

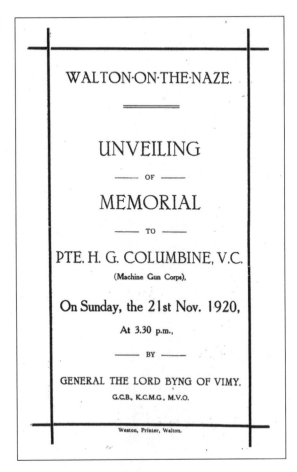

WALTON-ON-THE-NAZE.

UNVEILING

—— OF ——

MEMORIAL

—— TO ——

PTE. H. G. COLUMBINE, V.C.

(Machine Gun Corps),

On Sunday, the 21st Nov. 1920,

At 3.30 p.m.,

—— BY ——

GENERAL THE LORD BYNG OF VIMY.

G.C.B., K.C.M.G., M.V.O.

Weston, Printer, Walton.

At 9.35am 500,000 German soldiers advanced. Led by storm troopers with heavy machine guns, they used the thick fog and creeping barrage as cover. They made great advances through the 5th Army positions and had taken 21,000 British prisoners by the end of the first day. They were now only seventy-four miles from Paris. This was close enough to be able to fire their three Krupps cannons, the biggest artillery guns in the world. The shells from these huge guns would only take just over three minutes to reach the city and as 183 landed in Paris the population began to flee in panic.

Having grown used to three years of static warfare senior British military commanders had no idea what to do against this sudden German onslaught. Gough ordered the 5th Army to withdraw while the reserve was brought up

Local press coverage of the unveiling ceremony.

to cover the withdrawal. The attack on the 3rd Army to the north had made less progress, but British troops near Cambrai were nearly cut off. The Germans managed to push the British line back twenty miles and came dangerously close to achieving their objectives.

Bert and Francis, along with the rest of 9th Squadron Machine Gun Corps, had been moved into the Somme section a few days earlier. Here they were being held in general reserve waiting for the expected spring offensive.

As the German onslaught began the noise reached them several miles behind the lines. Bert had lived through several battles now and he knew this was no ordinary assault. The ground was trembling under the weight of the bombardment and visibility was steadily reducing as the air was filled with black acrid smoke and choking chlorine and mustard gas. Within minutes he and Francis had both put on their gas masks, grateful they weren't in the front line. Although the night was dark, the sky was lit up with the flames leaping from the 2,500 British guns as they replied to the German barrage.

By the 22 March it became obvious that all the reserves would be needed to halt the German attack. The Squadron moved to a new position near Montigny Farm, about seven and a half miles north-west of St Quentin and just over half a mile south of the village of Hervilly. The machine gun posts were set slightly in front of the main trench and to begin with Bert and Francis waited in the main trench, ready to act if the machine gunners were injured or killed. They had hardly had time to settle into their positions before the German infantry attacked in huge numbers. Bert had no time to think, as far as the eye could see there were swarms of grey blue field uniforms suddenly heading towards them. Before long they had taken the high ground and began firing on the men in the trenches behind him. Realizing the machine gunner in the trench in front of them was dead Bert didn't hesitate. Despite the heavy gunfire he rushed forward and took charge of the gun.

'Nothing I have seen or heard of could be finer than the heroism of this soldier. The enemy attacked suddenly in great force. They made considerable headway and from 'vantage ground' on either side they started to enfilade our trenches, causing severe casualties amongst the men. Part of our defence system included a machine gun post somewhat in advance of the main trench.

The men working this were all knocked out. Running the gauntlet of very heavy fire Private Columbine rushed forward and took charge of this gun. He was followed by some comrades, and, in spite of the fact that the whole of the enemy machine guns in the immediate neighbourhood concentrated their heaviest fire upon the post, which was almost unprotected by any of the devices commonly used, Columbine kept the machine gun going for over four hours.

At that time the enemy had been working round the position with strong forces, and actually had the post cut off, save for one narrow gap by which it was still possible to communicate with the main position. For the whole of the time, save when he went across the fire swept ground to bring ammunition, the brave chap remained at his post, and despite frequent rushes, he kept the enemy at bay. In the course of the fight, a German Officer appeared and repeatedly urged his men to the attack on the isolated post, but every rush of the Germans was stopped in a few yards by the deadly fire from this brave gunner who was actually wounded, but continued to work the gun in spite of that.

Early in the afternoon it became obvious that the position was hopeless and Columbine told the only two unwounded comrades left that it was folly for them to remain there. 'Save yourselves, I'll carry on' was what he said. They were reluctant to go, but he insisted and in the end they came to see the force of his contention that there was no point in sacrificing three lives where one was enough. He shouted a few words of farewell and that was the last his comrades heard from him.

From where we lay, we could see the fight going on, the swarms of grey-blue infantry around the position, the machine gun manned by the wounded hero, spitting out death. In the course of the hour, from noon to one, the enemy made eight attempts to rush the post. Each one was bought to a standstill. Therefore new tactics were necessary. Retiring to their position, the enemy concentrated heavy rifle and machine gun fire on the hero and his gun. At the same time a number of hostile aeroplanes appeared overhead. They were promptly engaged by our machines, but one detached itself from the fighting group and came down to about a hundred feet or so above the machine gun position, circling above for a few seconds like a great vulture ready to pounce on its prey.

We saw Columbine elevate his gun to attack his new enemy. The fight could only have one ending. A bomb was launched from the aeroplane, and there was a sharp report, gun and gunner blown up. The heroic fight of Columbine was not without its value, for the way in which he delayed the enemy attack gave us time to consolidate our position in the immediate neighbourhood, and when the enemy attacked, they found that the four hours' stand by this one man had put the German's plans hopelessly out of gear so far as capture of that series of positions was concerned. The comrades of the dead hero speak highly of him.

Dr PGC Atkinson (an eyewitness)[2]

Chapter 20

Sunday, 21 November 1920

The sound of *The Last Post*, played by the buglers of the 2nd Battalion Suffolk Regiment of Colchester, faded into the distance. Silence descended on more than 2,000 people who had gathered at the unveiling of the Columbine Memorial in Marine Gardens, Walton-on-the-Naze. Emma's fingers tightened their grip on her son's VC as she fought to hold back her emotions. All around her she could hear the muffled sounds of sobs of those who had also lost loved ones and she knew that for those precious minutes, she was not alone.

The afternoon had begun at 3.15pm with an inspection of local Ex-Service men by General Lord Byng of Vimy GCB, KCMG, MVO (former Commander of the 3rd Army). This was followed by a procession from the local church to the Marine Gardens. Coast guards, ex-Servicemen, Council members, Lifeboat men, Girl Guides, over 300 children of the elementary school, Freemasons, Buffalos, every organization in the town had been represented as the town paid tribute to Herbert. People had even come from Colchester and Clacton to honour her son.

On arrival in Marine Gardens they had sung a hymn, *Fight the good fight with all thy might* followed by a prayer from the Rev. W Harrison and a reading from the Scripture by Rev. E Bocok. Another hymn had followed, *God of our Fathers* and afterwards there was a statement from C F J Barker, Esq, Chairman of the Committee.

Then the memorial had been unveiled by Lord Byng and he had paid tribute to her son saying:

'Pte Columbine had won one of the finest Victoria Crosses that had ever been gained in any war. This distinction was hard to gain in the past war because deeds of gallantry took place almost every hour, therefore the award was all the more difficult to earn. But Columbine's deed stood out as one which perhaps even a Victoria Cross was scarcely adequate. What had Herbert Columbine stood for? In his opinion he stood for a great deal. Herbert Columbine represented the purist idealism that human nature could find. Pure idealism was that man's standpoint- pure idealism for his country, which made him stand for four hours in an absolute tornado of shellfire. The name of Herbert Columbine was one that he (the speaker) should ever cherish with the greatest feelings that man could give tongue too, as standing for the highest, purest and noblest idealism in the world.'

The memorial, designed and created by Mr N A Trent of London, was a simple bronze bust, its likeness taken from a photograph. It rested on a stone pillar. Under the bust a plaque bore the words:

> 'Pte H G Columbine V.C.
> Killed in action 22nd March 1918
> He refused to retire
> When he might have done so'

A second plaque, further down simply stated 'Erected by his Friends and Countrymen in ever grateful memory in the year 1920'. The unveiling was followed by a prayer from the Vicar (Rev. H C Knocker), and then the hymn *For all the saints*. As the hymn finished the air was filled with the haunting sounds of *The Last Post* and this was followed by a rousing chorus of *God Save the King*.

As the ceremony finished Lord Byng came over to Emma and spoke to her for several minutes, although afterwards she could never really recall what had been said. As he walked away, leaving her momentarily on her own, Emma suddenly felt lost. Then she felt her sister's gentle touch on her arm. Nodding inwardly, she touched the VC once more for courage and then gently laid her wreath with its poignant words 'To my darling son from his mother' at the foot of the memorial. Her sister Lottie laid her wreath next to Emma's 'In loving memory from Auntie Lottie, Keith and Annie' and then other people began laying their own wreaths to those they had lost. In a short while the whole of the area around the memorial was filled with wreaths to the fallen and then people were shaking her hand and congratulating her on having such a brave son.

As the crowd began to disperse Emma found herself unable to leave the memorial. The bust was such a good likeness that it was almost as if he were still with her and she resisted Lottie's initial attempts to take her home. As she stood there gazing at the bust she found it hard to believe that it was over two years since he had died, two years since she'd felt that her reason for living no longer existed. It was still a source of wonder to her that she had survived the dark days after his death and that, somehow, it had been the award of Herbert's Victoria Cross that had actually given her the courage to go on. Now, when she thought back, it was hard to remember the depths of despair she had sunk to or was it?

As she thought back she realized that she had no idea how she had survived the few days after that dreadful letter had arrived. She vaguely remembered everyone being very good, her neighbours taking it in turn to keep her company, cook her meals and generally look after her. She also remembered feeling very ungrateful, but all she had really wanted to do was to be left alone, to shout and scream and mourn her precious son. She had found it hard to stop herself yelling at them to go away and leave her alone.

Night times had been the worst. Alone with her thoughts she had relived the last time Bert had come home, over and over again. It had been so hard to believe that it was over two years ago since she had last seen him. If she closed her eyes tightly she could still see his smiling face telling her not to worry, that he would be alright and that the war would soon be over. Try as she might the tears would not come anymore. It was as if she had died inside and there was no more emotion, just an empty shell.

A few days later she had received the official army form, a bland acknowledgement of the death of her son that had left her feeling even more bereft than she had been after the original notification. It confirmed, as if she didn't already know, that to the army, Bert was just a number, nothing more.

'Madam, it is my painful duty to inform you that a report has this day been received from the War Office notifying the death of 50720 Private Columbine H G, 9th Machine Gun Squadron and I am to express to you the sympathy and regret of the Army Council at your loss. The cause of death

was killed in Action. Any application you may wish to make regarding the late soldiers effects should be addressed to 'The Secretary, War Office, Whitehall, London SW'

She was still seething about the impersonal army letter when a knock at the door made her jump. She glanced at the clock and sighed. It was probably only Annie with the post. She waited a few moments. Annie meant well, but she really couldn't face anyone else asking her if she was alright and looking at her with such sympathy that she wanted to scream. As soon as she heard the footsteps going away she walked to the front door. The letter was on the mat, in a bluff envelope, and Emma hesitated briefly before picking it up. Surely she had received all the official notifications now? When would they stop torturing her? She made her way back to her chair in the sitting room and sat looking at the letter for what seemed like ages, as she tried to make up her mind whether to open it. Eventually she decided that it couldn't possibly cause her any more pain than she was already in so she carefully tore it open. It was signed Lieutenant Eade 9 MG Squadron:

'Dear Mrs Columbine, you will no doubt have been informed by the War Office that No 50720 Private Columbine H G, is wounded and missing. He was in my sub-section, and although I had not the luck to be with him on 22nd March, I heard what happened from those who were there. He kept his gun firing to the last, although the Germans had got into the trench on both sides of him and were throwing bombs at him. In the end, he was seen to be hit by a bomb and very badly wounded. He was one of my best gun numbers, and is a great loss to the Squadron. I deeply sympathise with you, but it may be some consolation to you to know that he has been recommended for a medal in token of his bravery. It is the bravest deed I have ever heard of.'[1]

Emma frowned and then reread the letter again. She sighed, it was very nice to think that Bert was a hero, but wasn't it her telling him his father was a hero that had made him join the army in the first place. She didn't need reminding of it. Making up her mind she stood up and put the letter behind the clock. The priest would be here again soon, although why he kept coming was a mystery to her. She was already finding it hard to forgive God for taking both her husband and her only son and nothing he could say would make any difference. As for letters from officers, she didn't need someone telling her Bertie was a hero. To her Bertie had always been a hero; he didn't need to die to prove it.

Somehow she managed to get through the next few days. She tried to keep busy during the day, but most of her day to day tasks were now carried out in a trance. At night she would walk along the promenade until she was so tired she was able to find a few hours solace in sleep. It was her only comfort now, that and the first few waking seconds before the realization that Bert was dead, hit her again. Although it was now several days since she had first received the news, it still felt like a bolt of lightning, and the ensuing pain was just as fresh as it had been then. Those few seconds when she didn't remember were the only time she felt alive. Then it would be back to somehow enduring the day, and praying for the night, so she could go back to sleep again.

Other than her walks at night she had not been into the town. She couldn't face having to speak to people about Bert and having to accept their condolences. She wasn't sure she would be able to put a brave face on it in the face of their well-meaning sympathy. But it would be even worse if they didn't mention him at all for fear of upsetting her. Not speaking about him at all would be as if he had never lived.

As a Catholic it was sin to take your own life, but Emma found herself wanting nothing more than to go to sleep and never wake up. She tried praying, but God appeared to have gone deaf. He had taken her family, now he was ignoring her and the priest was unable to offer any real comfort. In fact Emma was relieved when he finally stopped calling every day as she had feared she might be rude to him and that would never do.

At least if she had a body to bury, a funeral to arrange, that might help alleviate the pain a little. It would at least feel like she was doing something for her precious boy. The thought of him not having a proper grave was almost more than she could bear. How could he rest in peace if his body had no resting place? She had asked the priest, but he had just muttered something about the soul being the part that went to Heaven not the body. It was all very well for him to say that, Bertie wasn't his son. It wasn't his beautiful son's body that was lying in the mud of France without a grave stone. How could she visit his grave if he didn't have one?

No longer feeling there was anything to live for she began to sink further into depression. With no funeral to arrange and having packed away all her clothes that weren't black there was nothing to do. She had only gone into

Bertie's room once since she'd heard about his death. She had hoped it would give her some comfort, but it was so long since he had lived there that she could no longer feel his presence. The room felt cold and empty, like her heart, so she closed the door firmly and vowed not to go back in there again. The help she was seeking was not there and, if it was not there, then it wasn't anywhere.

She closed her eyes and made one final attempt to pray. But the words would not come and eventually she gave up. A quick glance at the clock told her that the post was due and for a split second her heart leapt as she wondered if there would be a letter from Bertie. Then, as the expected knock on the door sounded, the reality of her situation rushed back in, crushing any hope she might have had that it had all been a bad dream. She buried her head in her hands. What on earth had she done to deserve so much pain, so much suffering? Why had God taken both her husband and her son from her?

As had become her custom lately, she ignored the knock and waited patiently for the footsteps to recede. After a few moments she went into the hall and was surprised to see three letters lying on the mat. The first was from Lottie, her sister, saying she would come and visit her at the weekend and the other two were from France. Surprised to receive more letters from France she opened them, almost without thinking. The first was from a Capt MacAndrews, Commanding 9th Sqn MGC. It began the same as the previous letter, offering her sympathy for her loss and then, just as she was about to put it down without reading the rest, something caught her eye.

'The news reached this brigade last night that the King has the pleasure of granting your son the Victoria Cross. He nobly earned the honour, his bravery and determination on the 22nd March are beyond words. This is the only VC that this brigade has had; in fact I think it is the only one the Division has had. I had a full parade of the Squadron this morning to read out the account of his action and also the letter of congratulation which we received from the General on behalf of the whole brigade of this very distinguished honour. In your loss of such a gallant son, you have the very deepest sympathy of every man in this Squadron, where he used to be so extremely popular. We all sincerely trust that your great sorrow may be to some extent lessened by your pride of his noble death, so noble that the King has honoured him with the very highest award.'[2]

Emma looked down at the letter and reread it. The Victoria Cross was the greatest award a soldier could be given and her son, her Bertie, had been awarded one. For the first time since she'd received the news that he was dead she felt a slight lifting of her mood.

She carefully put the letter aside and opened the second one.

'Dear Mrs Columbine, I do hope you will excuse me for taking the liberty of writing to you. But I feel I must write to you to sympathise with you for the terrible loss of your son, and to tell you how bravely he died. As I am the only one who got away alive, I feel sure you would like me to tell you about it. I am a very poor hand at writing but if it were possible for anyone else to see and feel as I do, they would understand how I feel about your son. He was the bravest man I have even seen in my life and no man on earth could possibly have given his life more bravely than he did, he never thought once of retiring when the others were doing so, and if he had chosen he could have got away. But we had lost both the Officer and Sgt in charge of us and no one else was left to give us orders so he stayed.

Well this is just what happened. He was No 1 on one gun and I was No 1 gun on the other, we were both in the same section and we were ordered to take up a certain position with our guns and gun teams which consisted of 5 men on each gun, we were given to understand that there were some of our own men in front of us. This however, was unfortunately not so, for, at about 8.30am we espied the Germans advancing to attack our trench. It is to be noted that we had no artillery support whatever. Bert saw them before I did and he shouted to me and we both opened fire and were able to hold them until about 1.30 although in front of Bert's gun there was no wire. I had wire in front of mine so I had a better chance than he. We had lost our Sgt in the first rush and our Officer was killed shortly after. Just after 1 o'clock we were repeatedly attacked by low flying aeroplanes which fired machine guns at us and the Germans also attacked at the same time. About 1.30 they made a very strong attack against us, and, as your son had no wire in front of him they were able to gain a strong footing in his trench on each side of him. I managed to check them, helped considerably by the wire round me.

Bert's position being now quite hopeless, he sent away the only two men who were left alive with him, both these men were severely wounded in getting away.

When I had, by continuous firing, somewhat checked the attack in front of my immediate position, I looked round to see how things were faring with your son. With the exception of a few yards in front of his gun, he was absolutely surrounded with Germans. He was firing furiously and inflicting terrible losses among the oncoming enemy and there were piles of dead and wounded all round him and in front. He kept working his gun until, suddenly, the inevitable happened, a bomb exploded with terrific force right in front of him and blew up both Bert and his gun. Mad with rage at the death of my dearly beloved pal, I swung my machine gun round and rapidly fired the remainder of my ammunition into the masses of Germans around him, and under cover of this temporary check, managed by great good fortune, to get clear away.

Oh! You have reason to be proud of your son dear Mrs Columbine, a braver man never lived than he, I could not have stopped there had it not been for his example. Through sticking there I have been awarded a bar to my DCM. I have just told what happened regarding your dear son and he has been recommended for the VC, and if ever a man on this earth deserved it, he did, he refused to retire when he might have done so and by his devotion to duty and his example to the rest of us, he was the means of holding up a large number of the enemy for about six hours and he died like a brave gunner should, with his gun and face towards the enemy.

Words fail me dear Mrs Columbine, to express the sorrow I feel for you in your terrible loss. I too miss him for he was my friend, but he left us an example which I for one, will never forget. I have a wallet with a letter and a post card that belonged to him, these I will send on to you. My address is 50773 F H Burke, 3rd Section, 9th MGS, BEF France.

I remain,
Yours sincerely,
F H Burke[3]

But Emma no longer saw the words on the letter. Instead, through the stream of tears that were pouring down her cheeks, she could see Bert clearly. He was standing to attention with his back to the fire, his uniform was pristine and his highly polished boots were gleaming in the light from the fire. But best of all, he was smiling at her and for the first time in days she smiled too. It seemed God had listened to her prayers after all. He had not forgotten her.

Notes

Chapter 1
1. *The Times* reported it as 'tea time' because it was 5pm when the Boer's ultimatum ran out.
2. Suzerainty refers to when one nation allows domestic sovereignty but controls another nation in international affairs
3. Commandos were locally raised detachments of all men in the electoral district who were old enough to carry a gun.

Chapter 2
1. A maltster selected cereals, mainly barley, from those growing in the fields that would be used for malting. Sometimes the barley would be grown on the brewer's own premises. The maltster would then modify the barley to the brewmaster's specifications so he could make a beer from it that had the flavour and alcohol content he wanted.
2. Joseph Swan invented the electric light bulb in 1878 and Thomas Edison invented an improved version in 1879.

Chapter 3
1. Sangars are trenches fortified with stone walls.

Chapter 4
1. It would appear that it was possible to apply for the pension even if the soldier had been killed before it had been introduced so it is likely Emma would have received it.
2. Although a wardrobe dealer could be someone who dealt in second hand furniture I also found a reference to a wardrobe dealer being a seller of second hand clothes.

Chapter 5
1. On the 1911 census it still refers to Walton as Walton le Soken.
2. A local landowner.

Chapter 6

1. They were called 'Lillywhites' because of their white busby-bags and white plumes.
2. The girl was known as 'a piece of square tack'.

Chapter 7

1. He rose from private to Field Marshal to become Quartermaster of the BEF in 1914 and Chief of Imperial Staff in 1915.

Chapter 10

1. Figures seem to vary depending on which sources you read.
2. 15th Brigade were part of II Corps and consisted of 'A' Squadron 19th Hussars (of which Bert was in), 1 Norfolk Regiment, 1 Bedfordshire Regiment, 1 Cheshire Regiment, 1 Dorsetshire Regiment, XV, XXVII, XXVIII, VIII, Brigade Royal Field Artillery, 108 Heavy Battery, 17TH, 59TH Field Company Royal Engineers.

Chapter 11

1. A saphead was a listening post which was normally a shallow, narrow position that was about thirty yards in front of the front line in no-man's-land, sometimes dangerously close to the enemy front line. They were used to gather intelligence on the enemy and to monitor activity.

Chapter 12

1. This would later be amended.

Chapter 13

1. The men called the Maxim QF 1 pounder gun a 'pom-pom' because it made a 'pom' sound when the shell left the German trench and another 'pom' when the shell landed in the British trench.
2. Pronounced 'Eepree'.
3. From General Headquarters at St Omer to all units, 24 December, 1914.

Chapter 14

1. Some sources believe that the name of the wood had nothing to do with Field Marshal Kitchener. Instead it is believed to be a literal translation of the original French name Bois de Cuisiniers – the wood of the cooks.
2. Two battalions of 80th Brigade consisted of 4th Kings Royal Rifle Corps and Princess Patricia's Canadian Light Infantry. The Princess Patricia's Canadian Light Infantry included a high proportion of former British regular soldiers, many of whom were Boer War veterans. The battalion was raised in 1914 and arrived on the Western Front in 1915.
3. 84th Brigade consisted of 1st Suffolk, 2nd Cheshire, 1st Monmouthshire, 2nd Northumberland Fusiliers.

Chapter 15

1. It had first been called Shell Trap Farm by the British but this was considered to be bad for morale so had been renamed Mouse Trap Farm.
2. These were based on hand-held weed sprayers used by gardeners.

Chapter 16

1. Unfortunately the individual records did not survive because the Register was never centralized. Instead the information was collected locally and the forms remained with the local registration authorities for as long as the Act remained in force which was until 1919. Some records were transferred to the General Register Office but in 1919, under the terms of the Public Records Act 1877, provision was made for the destruction of any records held either locally or by the General Register Office.
2. He had known Baker-Carr as a musketry instructor at Hythe.
3. Although the Vickers was adopted in 1912 it appears that only the cavalry machine gun sections were initially given the Vickers. Infantry machine gun sections were still using the Maxim. In my description of Mons I stated that Bert was using a Maxim this is because the various sources differ on which gun he would have been using at that time.
4. At the beginning of the war the Germans would warn merchant shipping that they were going to torpedo them, thus allowing the sailors and crew to escape but by 1917 they had pretty much stopped doing this. In 1917 alone over 3,000 merchant seamen were killed.

Chapter 17

1. In 1914 bread had been 6d, by 1917 it had risen to 11d.

Chapter 19

1. I have not been able to find out how many times Bert came home on leave but it is likely to have only been two or three times, if that.
2. © All letters and eyewitness account are courtesy of Graham Sacker, Machine Gun Corp (Old Comrades Association).

Chapter 20

1. © All letters and eyewitness account are courtesy of Graham Sacker, Machine Gun Corp (Old Comrades Association).
2. © All letters and eyewitness account are courtesy of Graham Sacker, Machine Gun Corp (Old Comrades Association).
3. © All letters and eyewitness account are courtesy of Graham Sacker, Machine Gun Corp (Old Comrades Association).

Postscript

The Great War finally ended in an armistice on 11 November 1918: it had lasted over four years and taken the lives of eight and a half million men. It was followed by the 1918/1919 influenza pandemic in which it is estimated that between twenty and forty million people died.

COPY

WARD C.2.

SOUTH WESTERN HOSPITAL,
LONDON ROAD,
STOCKWELL, S.W.9.

6.1.55.

Dear Sir,

Would it be possible for you to send my Nephew's (Pt. Herbert Columbine) V. C. to me.

I am ill in this Hospital and too ill to leave it. I am eighty three and would like to see it again.

I enclose a Postal Order for 2/- and will return the next day.

My Brother was killed in the South African War and Herbert was only six. I went to Buckingham Palace to receive it.

I would be so pleased to see it again.

Yours sincerely,

(signed) LOUIE COLUMBINE

P.S. I wanted to come to Walton to see it, but the Doctor said it would be too far, I cant walk.

Letter from Herbert's aunt requesting to see his medals before she dies.

RAR/P/M/3

10th January, 1955.

Dear Sir,

Private H. Columbine, V.C.

I enclose herewith a letter I have received from Mrs. L. Columbine, together with a Postal Order for 2/-, in connection with the Victoria Cross awarded to Private H. Columbine.

I enclose a copy of my reply to Mrs. Columbine, and no doubt you will communicate with her in due course.

Yours faithfully,

Clerk of the Council.

G. Lewis, Esq.,
Secretary,
British Legion Club,
Vicarage Lane,
Walton-on-the-Naze.

The letter was forwarded unto the Royal British Legion.

After news reached Walton that Herbert had died a collection was made for Emma, as she had refused an army pension. Small brochures were printed called 'The Deathless Story of an Essex VC' and sold for 2d. In the back, addressed to Major H K Newton MP, was a form for people to donate money. The money was sent to Mr Stanley Nicholson, Clerk to the Council, Town Hall, Walton-on-the-Naze.

The town raised £312-9s-2d, of this £10-5s-0d was given to Emma plus £200 in war bonds. By April 1919 there was £90-0s-6d in the bank towards a memorial.

Emma collected her son's posthumous VC on Saturday, 22 June 1918 from King George V at Buckingham Palace. Herbert's VC was reported in *The Times* on the 24 June as well as in all the local papers.

The response letting her know the request had been forwarded onto the RBL.

RAR/P/M/3

10th January, 1955.

Dear Madam,

Private H. Columbine, V.C.

Thank you for your letter of the 6th instant, in connection with the Victoria Cross awarded to Private H. Columbine.

The Cross is held by the British Legion Club at Walton-on-the-Naze, and I have therefore forwarded your letter and Postal Ord r for 2/- to the Secretary of the Club, who will no doubt write to you in this connection.

Yours faithfully,

Clerk of the Council.

Mrs. L. Columbine,
Ward C.2.,
South Western Hospital,
London Road,
Stockwell,
London, S.W.9.

When the Germans overran the area they buried all the bodies in one mass grave. Although this was later dug up at the end of the war, Herbert's body was never identified. His name is commemorated on the Pozieres Memorial, Panels 93 and 94. Pozieres is a village some 6km north-east of Albert. The memorial encloses the Pozieres British Cemetery, south-west of the village on the north of the main Albert to Pozieres road, the D929. The Memorial commemorates over 14,000 British casualties and 300 South African casualties with no known grave who died from 21 March to the 7 August 1918. It was unveiled in 1930 by Sir Horace Smith-Dorrien.

Emma Columbine's death certificate.

Walton-on-the-Naze's war memorial was also located on Marine Parade, fifty yards from the bust, but was later moved to the cemetery of the local parish church. It carried the names of the fifty-eight men from Walton who had also died in the Great War.

In a Council meeting held in October 1921:

> *'The Clerk reported that Mrs Columbine had offered to present the Council with the following medals belonging to her late son, in a case to be placed in the Council Chamber:- The Victoria Cross, The 1914 Star, The Victory Medal, The General War Medal, and the South African War Medal (belonging to her late husband). Moved by Councillor Pellatt, Seconded by Councillor Standley – That the Council be recommended to accept this offer with thanks. Carried.'*

The Council Meeting held on 25 January 1923 states:

> *'The case of medals which was promised to the council by Mrs Columbine was received. Moved by Councillor Kearns, Seconded by Councillor Jones – That*

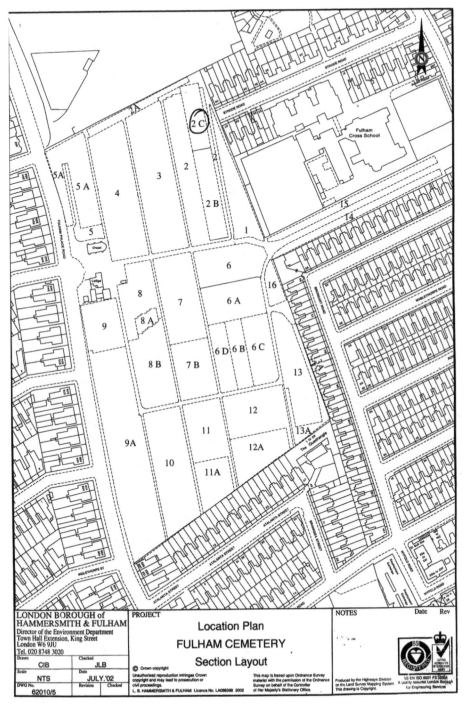

With little money Emma lies in an unmarked grave in Fulham cemetery.

the Clerk be instructed to write to Mrs Columbine expressing the Council's appreciation of this gift, and their cordial thanks to her for the same, and that this case be placed on the mantel shelf in the council chamber.'

In 1934 Walton Council amalgamated with Frinton Council. The medals were then handed to the local branch of the Royal British Legion for safe keeping. They were later put in a bank vault for security reasons and replicas put on display.

Emma remained in Walton-on-the-Naze until 1922 when she moved back to London to live with her sister, Lottie. The last address for Emma was 2 Hurlingham Road, Fulham. From here she was admitted to hospital with hypostatic pneumonia after a fall from her bed which fractured her femur on the 5 July 1945. She died on the 12 August 1945 and lies in an unmarked grave in Fulham Cemetery.

On the 6 January 1955 Louie Columbine, Bert's aunt on his father's side, wrote to the council and asked if they could send Herbert's VC to her so she could see it again before she died. Her doctor had refused her permission to go to Walton as she was too ill. She had collected her brother's (Bert's father) South African medal from Buckingham Palace when Bert was six and longed to see her nephew's medal one more time. She had enclosed a postal order for 2s to pay for the cost of postage. The letter and postal order was passed to the Royal British Legion who obliged by putting Herbert's VC in the post. It was returned to them a few days later with grateful thanks from Louie.

In 1970 the bust and plinth were vandalized and thrown in some scrub nearby. The bust had also been tossed into the sea on several other occasions. So it was decided to move it to Walton church as this was deemed to be safer. However in 1990 the bust was stolen. A replica was made but then the original turned up. It now stands in the Leisure Centre which bears his name.

Index